Selected Writings

Volume 3

A New Trinity

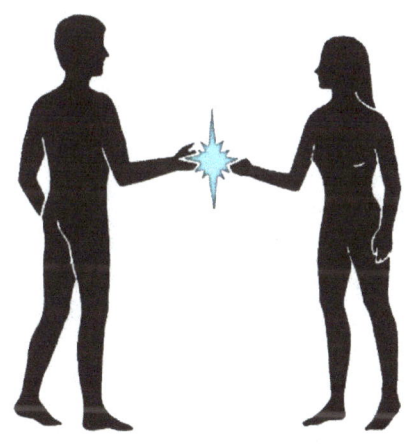

Christopher Alan Anderson

Selected Writings – Volume 3: A New Trinity
Copyright ©2025 Christopher Alan Anderson

ISBN 978-1506-914-75-6 PBK
ISBN 978-1506-914-76-3 EBK

June 2025

Published and Distributed by
First Edition Design Publishing, Inc.
P.O. Box 17646, Sarasota, FL 34276-3217
www.firsteditiondesignpublishing.com

ALL RIGHTS RESERVED. No part of this book publication may be reproduced, stored in a retrieval system, or transmitted in any form or by any means – electronic, mechanical, photocopy, recording, or any other – except brief quotation in reviews, without the prior permission of the author or publisher.

www.manandwomanbalance.com

Dedicated to:

Robert Daniel Birk

(March 1, 1950 - October 10, 2023)

Thank you, my friend, for bringing to my attention the writings of Walter and Lao Russell, (the University of Science and Philosophy), Ayn Rand, Kahlil Gibran, LifeSpring, A Course In Miracles, Meditation/Stillness, Raphael (Music to Disappear In); for being there solid as a rock when I was about to lose it on acid, and for the hundreds of phone calls we have had over the years discussing the metaphysics of the universe. Truly, you have been and will continue to be the definition of a friend!

"I am this moment!"

A note from the author:

Selected Writings--Volume 3: A New Trinity consists of some earlier writings that were side lined due to circumstances I was dealing with at that time. Recently, I was able to review them and found parts of those writings were quite pertinent, especially in the times in which we now live.

Both *A Love Perfected: The Coming Age of Spiritual Procreation* and *O Light Eternal: The Message of Eternal Life* were written sometime in the early 2000s, as was *Philosophical Investigations. A Life Given* was written sometime around or after 1998. I am adding Prefaces to each writing to help with the order. Also, I have added a few new sections toward the end of each writing to bring them more up to date. The epilogue consists of five selections from *Meditations for Deepening Love,* an already published writing.

I use a number of quotes in my writings, both from other writers as well as from my earlier writings. If a quote is from another writer, I include the author's name. If you see a book title and quote but no author listed, you can assume the author is myself and I am quoting from one of my other writings.

C.A.A.— June 21, 2024

Contents

A Love Perfected: The Coming Age of Spiritual Procreation 1

Philosophical Investigations 63

A Life Given 118

O Light Eternal: The Message of Eternal Life 161

Epilogue: Meditations for Deepening Love 230

A Love Perfected: The Coming Age of Spiritual Procreation

Preface

A Love Perfected: The Coming Age of Spiritual Procreation presents to us the idea of Spiritual Procreation. In our world today procreation is associated with the idea of "Begetting to bring forth offspring." (Merriam-Webster) Another word related to procreation is reproduction. Clearly, the procreation/reproduction of life is necessary for LIFE. Most of us understand this organically within ourselves. But if I were to suggest to you that procreation also works on the mental level as contrasted to the physical level many would question that or not understand what is meant by that. I mean, don't both male minds and female minds work the same? Do they?

But let's take that a step further with the suggestion that procreation/reproduction works not just at the physical and mental levels but on the spiritual level as well. What is that to mean? We generally equate the spiritual level with things such as salvation, forgiveness, perfection, enlightenment, illumination, eternal life, etc. Surely, a one God, Source, I AM, etc., must be our Living Center. But is it? In this writing, I am presenting a different view of what constitutes our Living Center. I am calling it Spiritual Procreation and, furthermore, with this as our Living Center we will finally be able to experience—***a love perfected***.

Contents

What is Spiritual Procreation?

Why is this Message Coming to Us Now?

The Conceptual Shift—From a One-Force Universe to a Two-Force Universe

Male and Female

The Procreation of Life

The Four Explanative Drawings of Spiritual Procreation

Original Sin Versus Spiritual Perfection

Spiritual Procreation and Eternal Life

What is Spiritual Procreation?

Spiritual procreation is an absolute. In fact, it is the one absolute of the universe. It might be called a metaphysic, construct, structure, or frame. It can be thought of as an order, constant, principle, or law. It is "what is," i.e., *the Given*.

Given that spiritual procreation is "what is," it can be said that it is universal. This is to say that spiritual procreation operates everywhere at all times. There isn't any place or "reality" whereupon spiritual procreation is not functioning. In all our lives, it is operating *right now*. Spiritual procreation centers life. Whenever or wherever there is life, there is spiritual procreation.

Spiritual procreation (whatever that may be) is always connected to life. Our only concern here is *life*. We ought not to be interested in anything that is not pertinent to life. That may seem obvious to some, but apparently not to all. Since the "beginning of time," mankind has been hanging his or her hat (basing his or her life) on various metaphysical structures/belief systems that are not pertinent to life. There is not one religion in the world today that is fully centered in life. Spiritual procreation will correct that.

Spiritual procreation does not deny the necessity of a belief system. A belief system is nothing more than a conception of reality. All of us must hold within our minds a conception of reality. It, conception, is the mechanism whereby we are (or can be) conscious. Spiritual procreation as a conception of reality serves as an anchor for consciousness itself. Because it exists (as an absolute given), we can be conscious of "what is." Consciousness itself cannot be anything other than a conscious of "what is." Given that spiritual procreation is "what is" (which will be shown as we proceed), it can be said that consciousness is nothing other than being conscious of spiritual procreation itself.

But is spiritual procreation just another belief? Yes and no. It is a conception of reality. It is also the universal mechanism through which life operates. Spiritual procreation is as real as life. We would not want to say that a newborn baby is just another belief system, would we? That baby is *life*, and we can *know, experience,* and *feel* this baby as life (with all the *life* attributes attached to him or her) because we are (or can be) conscious due to the order/conception of spiritual procreation which is nothing other than life itself. *Life is our conception/experience that gives to us our understanding /meaning of life in life.* Life is "what is."

    I understand that I have yet to specifically answer the question of this chapter, *What is Spiritual Procreation?* That actually is the question of this whole writing and will require more than this one chapter to answer. In this section, I only want to lay a foundation— *Spiritual procreation is the given of life.* It is the universal and absolute. It is the understanding or reference whereby we are or can be conscious of life and its workings. And most of all, it is as real as a newborn baby because spiritual procreation is the actual (conscious) connection and expression of life, one to another.

Why is this Message Coming to Us Now?

The necessity of survival. That is why this message is coming to us now. We are no longer able to survive on our past understandings (belief systems). It is as if our past/current internal programming is incapable of ensuring our success. A (paradigm) shift embracing spiritual procreation is paramount.

E.F. Schumacher (1911-1977)—*Small Is Beautiful*
"The *modus operandi* of any economy—and the way in which the *modus operandi* was studied, interpreted, and judged—was derived from, and dependent upon, the religious and philosophical foundations of the culture in which it operated."

We could say the *"modus operandi"* (working order) of Life *"was derived from, and dependent upon, the religious and philosophical foundations...."* What if those religious and philosophical foundations don't match up to the **Given of Life**? How would we even know? What is our basis for knowing? Is knowledge axiomatic (self-evident)? Does existence exist? Is life a primary? At some point we will have to say *"Yes."* Perhaps that will be our starting point—into the shift of spiritual procreation.

For this shift to occur, an obstacle must be overcome. That obstacle is our own past/current belief systems. I have stated that a belief system, by its nature, is not the problem. Each of us must have a conception of things in order to be conscious. Belief itself may be the most powerful force in the universe. It is premised in the desire/need to be conscious, <u>to live</u>. Even if one's belief system is misconstrued (or even irrational), one will cling to it. The belief system holds one's mind (order) in place. Yet, for one to take on a new order (such as spiritual procreation), an altering or perhaps total restructuring of one's belief system is required. This altering or restructuring is not necessarily an easy thing to do. In fact, it is the challenge of our very survival.

But why embrace spiritual procreation? Is it somehow equivalent to "the truth"? And, even if it is, haven't all truth claims been discredited due to ideological bias? In answer to this last question, in a way, *"yes."* The philosophical pursuit of (metaphysical) truth collapsed some hundred-plus years ago for this very reason. It was "concluded" that "the truth" could never be separated from personal bias, i.e., that there was always a motive or vested interest (such as one's survival) in play in anyone's truth claim. For example, if one were to claim that "God exists," we now would have to ascertain the "hidden agenda" one has in play for making that claim. Today, we might have to check out the religion, ethnicity, political persuasion, or gender orientation of the one making the claim to see if it is politically/socially correct! There might be a disguised quest or claim for power and control over another in play, might there not?

But let us follow this through. If all truth claims are simply hidden agendas for power and control (to fulfill survival needs), what about those who proclaim this exact (and immensely popular) notion? Are we to believe these "subjectivists" or "relativists" who claim there isn't any absolute truth, only subjective or relative truth, and that all truth claims are tainted by their nature? Is this true? Are these relativists somehow more knowing in mind and pure in heart and thus free of any ulterior motive for their (truth) claim that "all truth claims are tainted and those making them are suspect?" Are we now to believe that those who stand for nothing (or perhaps everything) are somehow free from the personal (survival) bias they claim surround those who take a stand or hold a position? In short, are we any better off in today's climate that offers us the "truth of no truth" than we were in holding to the dogmas of the past?

An essential aspect of spiritual procreation is that it returns us to the framework of an absolute. Do we have any choice? Collapse is all around us. The center cannot hold because, after all (according to the relativists), there isn't any center! Must we be careful that this idea of spiritual procreation is not turned against those who may choose to embrace something else? Of course. One of the remarkable things about spiritual procreation is that it presents to us (for the first time) the framework for the sanctity and sovereignty of each and every individual life, i.e., *unalienable rights for all,* irrespective of personal belief. Can we make that same claim of our past/current belief systems, including the subjectivist's belief that "the only absolute is that of no absolute?" No, we cannot. We think we are so free and advanced in mind. In reality, we have yet to seriously look into the light. Now we must, irrespective of how bright it may shine. Why? Because of the necessity of survival. Our very lives do depend on it.

The Conceptual Shift: From a One-Force Universe To a Two-Force Universe

Sometime ago a shift* occurred in the mind of mankind. This shift created consciousness as we know it today. Before this shift, mankind had been in a pre-conscious or instinctive state, bound "inside of nature." This pre-conscious man (men and women) was not necessarily aware of his unique existence—*I am*. What consciousness consisted of was more of a group, tribal, or collective consciousness rather than a sense of self (individuality). Undoubtedly, what necessitated this shift were the survival pressures of the time. The pre-conscious mind can only integrate so much before it reaches its limit and can no longer adequately organize the growing survival demands.

*The Origins Of Consciousness In The Breakdown Of The Bicameral Mind—Julian James, 1973; The Riddles of Philosophy—Rudolf Steiner, 1914; The Dawn of Conscience—James H. Breasted, 1933

This shift from pre-consciousness or group/collective consciousness into a sense of self or individuality opened the door to cognitive or reflective thought—*I know that I am*. It occurred through conception, more specifically the abstraction of a one order (reality). Imagine yourself being bound by this pre-conscious nature. You cannot see (conceive of) it as you are "inside" it. Suddenly, seemingly out of nowhere, you conceive (consciously experience) in your "mind" an order to things. (You don't necessarily know what this order is, only that there is an order.) Now, instead of being "bound by nature," you find (through conceptualization) nature to be bound by you. You become conscious of nature. Yes, you are still in it per se, but your conceptualization of it places you in relation or contrast to it. The contrast is an apparent separation or distinction between you and nature. What arises from this (self-other) distinction is *I am*. You now stand *conceptually* separate from nature as a unique conscious individual. You are conscious that you are conscious of yourself in contrast to the otherness around you. (Self and other always come together.) It is from this shift into a *self-consciousness* that there arose in mankind the capacity to individually contemplate, reflect, decipher, conclude, decide, reason, i.e., *to think*. Thinking was the grand result of the paradigm shift from pre-consciousness to self-consciousness and, although we tend to take thinking for granted, it was this unique ability of self-conscious man (men and women) that has made the world as we know it today.

This shift into self-consciousness was given a name—*monotheism*. (At least, that is one name for it.) We usually think of monotheism in religious terms, emphasizing the existence of a *one God*. From a cognitive perspective, the emphasis here is on the idea *one*, not on "God." Metaphysically speaking, monotheism refers to or infers a **one order**. It is this consciousness (or abstraction) of a one order (that gives to us the self-other distinction and sense of "I am") that we hold today. Our consciousness is that of the *individual self*. This progression or shift from pre-consciousness to individual or self-consciousness was and is an absolutely necessary step in the evolution of consciousness, of life. In fact, without the conception of a one order to abstract self from other, we would not be conscious of self—or other. Everyone who is individually conscious has made this abstraction whether conscious of it or not. In the evolution of consciousness and the survival of life, no one can sidestep this consciousness shift that brings each one of us into a consciousness of oneself.

Unfortunately, there was a flaw or misconception in this shift from pre-consciousness to individual consciousness. It is not that this shift was not necessary, but that it was not complete. The (individual) consciousness or context we hold (of ourselves, of the world, or of "God") today is not metaphysically adequate or accurate. It was not structured correctly at its inception and, therefore, we are not able to conceive/perceive clearly. It is as if all of our thinking and experiencing is inherently flawed or distorted going in, yet we don't or can't see that. The majority of us just take our thinking for granted as if by some automatic process what we conceive/perceive is exactly "how it is." We tend to think our conception of things is complete. We don't question the structure of our thinking or the premises we arrive at. In short, we fail to understand that the shift from pre-consciousness to individual consciousness was a very important step but not a final step in the evolution of consciousness.

But why would this shift from pre-consciousness to individual consciousness, if so necessary, have embedded within it a flaw that would distort and misguide our very thinking without our knowing? The answer lies in a deeper understanding of the idea of monotheism. For example, when we think of the idea of a "one God," implied in that conception is a one order—the first abstraction of consciousness. So far so good. But "order" is not the only abstraction or implication available or necessary in the monotheistic conception. There is another *primary category* to consider. When we think about "God" (or the universe), we also bring into play the idea of a first cause, creator, or prime mover, i.e., *a primordial force.* **Force** is the other primary category in our first conception of "God" or Creator. We might say there is an order (conceptualization) and there is a force (actualization). The monotheistic conception did not exclude force per se; "God" was viewed as both the metaphysical or divine order and the <u>primary or creative force</u>. To be more accurate, the monotheistic shift (from pre-consciousness to individual consciousness) was actually built on the dual assumptions of a one order and a one force. This one order/one force structure or meta-stratum is the inner control of our consciousness, the essence of our conception of "God" or Creator, and is the controlling force in the world today. Literally, it directs and controls our cognitive faculty (minds) from which we conceive and perceive.

It is from this understanding (of one order/one force) that we now can view the flaw or misconception that confronts us. The problem simply is that there isn't any nor can there ever be a one singular primordial creative force. Yes, there can be a "one" order as order is a conception or representation of things. But there cannot be a one (singular) force. Why not? Because force, by its very nature, is *relational* or *oppositional*. The whole context of the mechanism or manifestation of force is force/counter-force. **Force exists part and parcel as a relation of forces.** Every school child knows "that for every action there is an equal and opposite reaction." For every force there is a counter-force or polar opposite. *Every singular force exists in a context or a duality of forces.* Just as we cannot have one side of a coin without the other or have day without night or inhalation without exhalation, so we cannot have a singular force without its ever-present counter-force. *There is not nor can there ever be a singular primordial force of creation.* "God," as a singular force, does not exist. But there can be **two** primordial forces.

Imagine, for thousands of years (since the dawn of consciousness), mankind has been living in a conceptual frame that is not accurate to life. All of our conceiving/perceiving has been running through this one order/one force filter that, by its very nature, distorts reality. Thus, we (you and me) aren't really able to get to the heart of things. We are blocked from touching the source of life by an unconscious assumption/distortion in our filter system that we call the mind. We don't even know that we do not and cannot know from our current perspective of things.

Now, let's take another step and imagine changing our filter system to a structure of one order/two forces. Such a change would actually constitute a fundamental (paradigm) shift. It is a shift at the most basic metaphysical or root level of consciousness. This is the shift that is actually occurring today. Granted, it is mostly unconscious but the signs are there. And this shift is just as dramatic (and necessary) as the shift from pre-consciousness to individual consciousness that occurred some four-thousand plus years ago. This shift is from a 1st order or one-force (singular) consciousness to a 2nd order or two-force (relational) consciousness that not only (existentially) recognizes *"I am,"* but also recognizes *"You are."* We have not truly been conscious of each other, *the You*. We should have been. You (the other) shows up with the first abstraction of a one order creating the self-other distinction. But the other (you) collapsed in the one-force mis-premise. Let's recognize both of us *equally* and *primordially* in the understanding of a **two forces of creation**. This is the shift—a shift that will affect and literally uproot religion, philosophy, psychology, sociology, science, economics, politics, government, art, education, family, everything. You see, our whole world has been premised in the idea of a "one primordial force." Now, that (faulty) premise is being uprooted and a new correct premise of a **two primordial forces** is taking its place. We might just say that this Universe in which we live is put a *polarity/interaction* between forces. This paradigm shift from a one (singular) force to two (relational) forces will require that each one of us (spiritually) surrender everything we think we have or are.

The Evolution of Consciousness

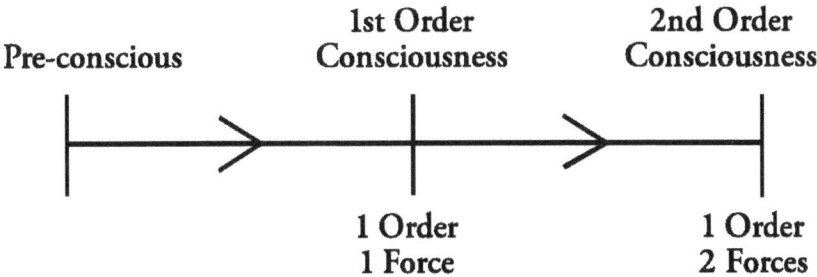

In review then, the consciousness shift necessary for our survival begins with the distinction between order and force. This simple distinction, with its implication of a two primary forces (rather than one), moves us from a metaphysics of singularity or independence to that of relationship or *interdependence*. This sense of relationship (You are and I am) is what can be called a ***2nd order consciousness***. Instead of viewing ourselves individually, as if we somehow exist by or for ourselves alone, we begin to view ourselves as part of a relationship with another (force). Similarly, we would no longer view the universe or "God" as some primordial singular force or creator. We have to make the leap to the reality of *two primordial forces*, not just one. Am I suggesting that there isn't any "God"? Not singularly. Whatever exists, exists as part of or through a relationship with something else, i.e., force/counter-force. Whatever name you want to give to "it" such as God, spirit, Tao, ether, cause, source, substance, essence, being, force, energy, mind, creator, etc., *there are two of them*. There just isn't a one singular primordial creative force in (or out) of the universe! *There are two forces*. Do you see the distinction and shift?

Within a few short pages, you have been presented with an evolution of consciousness going from pre-consciousness to a one-force (1st order) consciousness to a two-force (2nd order) consciousness. This evolution is made possible by a simple distinction between order and force that for some reason was not made at the dawn of consciousness (age of monotheism). We can speculate as to why not but, more importantly, it is now being made and from this shift (from one order/one force to one order/two forces), the door is being opened into the heart of spiritual procreation for all to see. Spiritual procreation does not exist in a one-force universe (which is a mis-premise). It only exists in a universe of *two forces*.

The following quote is from my earlier writing *The Discovery of Life*.

The Discovery of Life © 1994

For aeons, mankind has been caught in a trap, a trap so hideous it has prevented men and women from achieving any type of enduring success. Yet, from this trap our religions formed and promised mankind a way out through another world. Later, our socio-political institutions were formed, promising us liberation in this world. Yet, neither could deliver, for they were part of the trap, which was nothing but a simple misconception mankind made at the dawn of consciousness preventing him/her from discovering life.

This writing is about understanding and correcting that misconception whereupon mankind, for the first time, may discover life, thereby bringing a fulfillment and completion to his (or her) self/life.

Male and Female

Mankind has just arrived at the point in the evolution of consciousness where we now can understand that the creative center of the universe (what historically has been called "God") is, in fact, not a one (force) but a two (forces). This is to suggest that the absolute order of the universe does not consist of a singular "creative" force but rather is a plurality (or polarity) of *co-creative* forces. These two forces, whatever they may be, always come together. *They comprise a relationship.* There isn't any state of existence whereby one exists (or can exist) by him or herself alone. **Existence is always a co-existence.** As the Jewish philosopher/mystic Martin Buber (1878–1965) once said, *"All real living is meeting."* Life exists in a relationship, a meeting with another. A single force by itself alone is not living. Only a universe of two forces is alive.

Relationship, by its nature, has certain primary characteristics. One of these characteristics is that the two parts are *equal* to each other. By equal I mean *equal-in-necessity* to the survival or existence of the whole relationship. Both parts of the relationship are *equally necessary*, not only for their own survival but for the survival of the other as well. There actually is a co-dependence in play. We use the more correct term *interdependence* today, but it actually means co-dependence. Take breathing, for example; inhalation is absolutely dependent upon exhalation for its survival. It is dependent on itself as well, and equally, exhalation is dependent upon inhalation. Do you see the interdependence or *balance* in play? Oftentimes, we consider ourselves "singularly independent," thinking we do not need anyone else. But we do need another for our very survival. And, equally, that other needs us as well.

Sometimes we acknowledge the reality of relationship but do not hold to the equality of the two parts. We might think of ourselves as a little more important than or "superior" to the other. Or we might think the other is superior and we are "inferior." In either case, the relationship is imbalanced. These imbalanced relationships are known as *hierarchical relationships* and exist throughout religion

(Original Sin, the Trinity, the Virgin Birth, and the Chosen People) and government (the Divine Right of Kings [Fascism] or the Sovereignty of Government over the People [Communism]. Hierarchy has been the basis of patriarchy (men superior to women) and racism (the white race superior to the black race) that we are so familiar with. These imbalanced types of relationships always result in one part claiming some type of power and privilege over another. The essence of the hierarchical relationship is *master/slave* because one fails to see the equal necessity of the two parts. Metaphysically speaking, *no one is greater than another; no one is lesser than another*. It is important to understand that until one makes the discovery of a **two forces of creation**, he or she will be stuck in hierarchy. The one-force flaw or misconception always results in hierarchical imbalance (I am greater—or lesser—than you). With this understanding of the balance of the two forces, we can finally step beyond metaphysical hierarchy.

The other primary characteristic of relationship is that of difference. Many people today actually agree with what I have said about "our equality." They have a more difficult time with "our difference," thinking perhaps that difference suggests stereotyping and judgment. But let me ask you, are we the same? I mean, if everything was exactly the same, there would be no-thing, <u>no individual thing</u>. All individual uniqueness (difference) would collapse into sameness (nothingness). Life as we know it is built on both equality (I am equal to you) and difference (I am not you). This is not to deny some sort of "oneness" we may have together, but it is to say that "oneness," whatever that is, is never by itself alone. Oneness, or what I would rather call *unity*, exists only in relationship to twoness or *division*. Twoness, of course, is in relationship to oneness. These terms do not have any meaning by themselves alone. They themselves comprise the two equal but *different* aspects of relationship. Ultimate reality is not some sole unity or separate individuality; it is both. All of us exist in a state of relationship, equal to yet different from one another.

The historical term given to this idea of difference is *opposition*. Think of the two as polar opposites. An example of polar opposites is breathing—inhalation and exhalation. Notice that there must

always be this fundamental two. We can say that two primordial forces exist and that they are equal to but opposite from each other. Do you see that? Equal and opposite is the structure or frame of the whole universe. Everything that exists does so within this frame. Reality is
not some cosmic swirl of non-differentiated oneness (nothingness) nor is it some compartmentalized individual separation from which the two can never interact (touch). Rather, it is a relationship between polar opposites who are both connected but separate, united but divided, equal but opposite. In short, you exist in relation to your equal but opposite, i.e., *other half*, right now. You always have and always will, just as will I.

The Structure of the Universe

Equal and Opposite

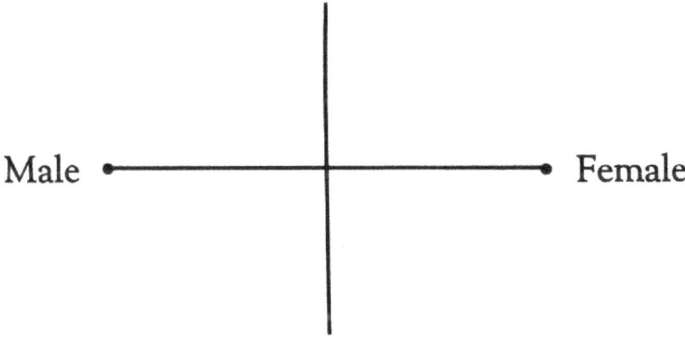

There is another name we give to this idea of difference or opposition and that is *sexuality*. To say, for example, that male and female are sexual is only to say that they are different from or opposite of each other. (Or we could say that they are different and, therefore, sexual.) Sexuality is nothing more than difference. Metaphysically speaking, all difference is sexual difference. Sexuality exists in the universe as its structure. This is simply because there are two (equal but opposite) forces. This idea of a structural sexuality is important. Sexuality is not secondary to some greater cause as if it is just limited to our physicality or biology. No, sexuality is metaphysical, embedded in the exact nature of the universe as the universe. **This is a sexual universe of two (equal but opposite) forces.** Every individual thing in it is sexual, operating in relation with its sexual opposite. Yin and yang not-withstanding, our religions and philosophies fail to view the sexual as metaphysical. The metaphysical or *spiritual* has a nature, but it is not a "one force" as most of us think. There are *two forces*. But how can we see that, and the implications of that, if we are holding to a metaphysic of one order/one force?

Each one of us exists as a sexual being. We exist either as a male or a female. There really aren't any other options. Moreover, we exist in a primary relationship with each other. Male is a male *in relation to a female*. Female is a female *in relation to a male. We sexually exist in relation together. All existence is sexual existence; male or female*. We really don't exist as both sexes as if there is some type of inner bisexuality or androgyny. Yet, this is a popular notion today. Many believe that although we may be sexual beings physically that spiritually we are bisexual or perhaps of no sex. Somehow, we are to believe, that the two-force sexual process disappears in the spiritual domain. It doesn't. In the spiritual world, if you want to call it that, a male is a male in relation to a female and a female is a female in relation to a male. Wherever there is existence there is sexual opposition. The reason why we have failed to see this is because of the one-force mis-premise. We think spiritually that everything is one. Thus, we fail to consider the two forces of male and female as primary and, moreover, fail to understand the essential purpose/function of male as to female in the universe. What is a male actually? What is a female? Why are there males and females? How is their interaction together necessary for survival? These are the types of questions we ought to be asking, questions of our **sexual identity**. Foremost, we need to know who we are **sexually**.

To understand the essential questions of existence (What is male? as to What is female?), we must look into the dynamic interaction of these two sexual forces. We know they exist together in a relation of equal but opposite. We know they are dependent upon each other which means they each have something the other *existentially* needs. Well, what is it that a male needs that only a female can give him? What does a female need that only a male can give to her? Let's look into the sexual dynamic and see what we can discover.

What is Male?

What is Female?

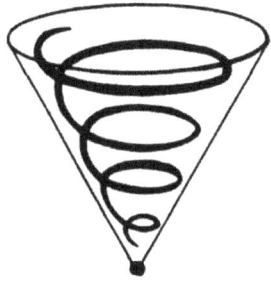
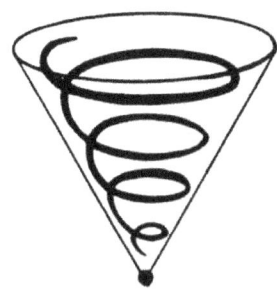

In the sexual act, the male seeks to penetrate the female. His desire is to release himself into her. His action constitutes giving himself over to her. Conversely, the female seeks to be penetrated. There is a fusion or unity that takes place between the two. Her desire is to receive the male into herself. The separated two become as one, if you will, only to become as two again. This sexual process is continuous, each part bringing on the desire for the other. This sexual process is the life process. **Life is sexual interchange**. There isn't any escaping it. There isn't any escaping our sexuality in relation to our sexual opposite. There aren't any other worlds or realities to flee to. There is only male and female in uniting and dividing interaction together.

Now, if you think about it, the sexual dynamic doesn't stop there. What the man has placed within the woman (if it unites with her) begins to grow inside of her and, in time, she gives birth to a new *sexual* life. The "one" has separated into another "divided two." We call this process the *reproduction* or *procreation* of life. The sexual dynamic is a process or interaction between division and unification. Said simply, *the one divides and the two unite*. Division of the one is into the polar opposition of male and female. Unity of the two by the polar opposites voids or rests the opposition (in potential) creating the dynamic for the next division. Again, think of the breathing cycle. From inhalation comes exhalation, creating the need for inhalation and so on. The process or cycle is in a dividing/uniting (sexual) interaction together that goes on forever.

The Sexual Process

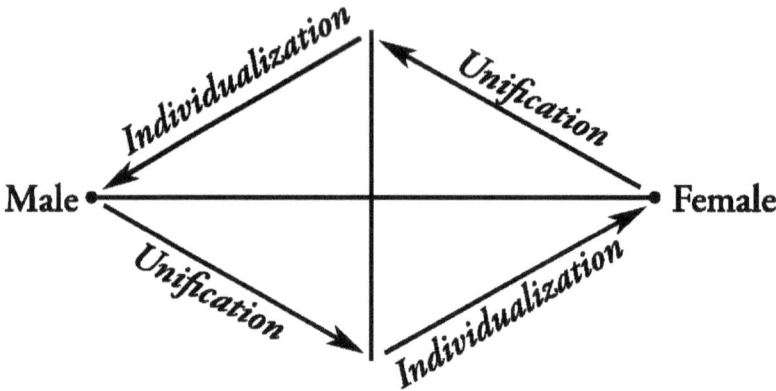

This sexual dynamic or process (of division and unification) between the two forces of male and female is the process of all life. The whole process or cycle of life is one of *birth-life-death-rebirth*.... The division of the one is that point of birth into sexual form, male or female. Birth is what we call the beginning point of life. The unification of the two into one is actually what we call death. Death is but a resting point and it occurs at every sexual release (exhalation). Death is that release of individual sexual form. Each sexual release constitutes a life (individual) surrender into the unity from which we have come. From death comes forth the next sexual expression (or reproduction) of life—a rebirth. The new birth will, of course, be into sexual form, male or female. All of life is expressed sexually, male or female. All of death is a release of that sexual compression. Think of a tire being blown up; that is life or sexual compression. Sexual release or decompression is when the air is being released from the tire. After the air has been released it, the tire can again be blown up. Birth-life-death-rebirth... is the sexual/life cycle that each one of us is inscribed in with our equal and opposite other half. This whole cycle I often just refer to as *life* or perhaps *eternal life*.

Life

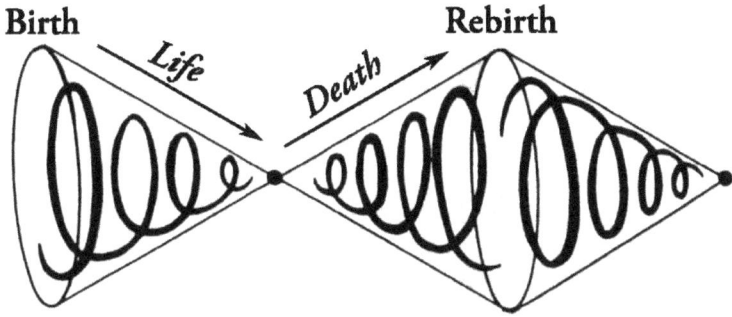

I probably should add a clarification here concerning the idea of oneness. We oftentimes think of oneness/unity as something different than sexual unity, as if it is somehow outside of the sexual process. It isn't. It is just *one parameter point* of the sexual process. Oneness is not even sexually neutral. It is sexed potential, male or female, at rest. Let us remember, there isn't any "outside" of the sexual process. There isn't any non-sexual existence. There is though, a male and a female dividing apart and uniting together over and over again.

Now, we can use other terms to express the sexual process that will help us grasp this universal process of opposites. I have used inhalation and exhalation. What are other opposites that you can think of? How about effort and rest. Can you see the process in play? Effort is fatiguing and brings on the desire to rest. Rest is rejuvenating and brings on the desire to again effort. And so it goes, *the two-force process of creation*. Let's list some more opposites and, as we do, ask yourself which side you think male corresponds to and which side female corresponds to.

Opposites

Division	Unity
Individuality	Universality
Material	Spiritual
Twoness	Oneness
Point	Field
Consciousness	Existence
Inhalation	Exhalation
Effort	Rest
Sound	Silence
In	Out
Gravity	Magnetism
Compression	Expansion
Tension	Relaxation
Charge	Discharge
Power	Direction
Success	Connection
Reason	Intuition
Security	Reproduction
First Say	Final Say

Let's now return to the essential questions of this section—What is male? as to What is female? We can now ask the question in this way as well: *Do you divide the one or do you unite the two?* This is the great (metaphysical) question of our sexual identity. If you are a male, you will do one of these tasks; if you are a female, you will do the other. All males do the same function; all females the opposite function. That is what male and female are—*opposites*. If the idea of "dividing the one" and "uniting the two" seems too abstract to you, think of the universe as a great big ship. Now a ship needs a motor to power it and a rudder to guide it. Who is the motor, male or female? Who is the rudder, male or female? Whichever function one sex does, the other sex will do the opposite. We don't do both although some of us may like to think we do. We may help each other but our core sexual function, *our essential defining difference*, lies in our (sexual) opposition not in our similarity or sameness. In spirit we, male and female, are opposites.

Why is this question of our *sexual identity* so important? Well, for one reason, until we know who we *sexually* are, we cannot fully or consciously unite together. It is from the understanding of our sexual difference that we can recognize just how much we need each other in this enterprise called *life*. When we can (spiritually/sexually) embrace each other in the understanding of *our life together*, we begin to open the door to spiritual procreation. Spiritual procreation begins with the sexual understanding of the two forces of male and female in their sexual uniqueness (opposition) and need for each other. So let us answer the questions—What is male? as to What is female? in the two forces of creation. The following quote is from my writing *The Two forces of Creation* which constituted a metaphysical shift for me.

The Two Forces of Creation © 1988—Selected Writings, Volume 2 © 1991, 2010

Male is that force which seeks to individualize a form separate and apart from the unity of male-female. The male desire is to hold male and female in individual form. It is the active conscious effort of holding separate (sexual) identity in relation to the other. The male effort is simply to hold apart and stabilize the man and woman relationship. We call this the effort to secure Individual form or just *security*.

Female is that force which seeks to unite the division of male and female. The female desire is to unite the separate male and female forms together as one. She rests the man and woman relationship through unifying the male within herself. It is from this unity that the next division or reproduction of life can take place. The female effort then is to unite the separate forms of male and female, resting the separate forms in unity so that the next reproduction of sexual form will take place. We call this resting of old form/begetting of new form *reproduction*.

In essence, it is the male effort to secure form and the female effort to reproduce form that makes for life and its continuity. Each aspect makes for one half of their creative process. Yet, and this is an important point, neither aspect can complete their creative desire without the other. The male cannot continually secure form. That effort is fatiguing and brings on a desire to rest. It is at this point that the male takes what he has secured in form and gives it over to female. The male deposits his life seed (force) into a female, releasing his form into her from which his next reproduction, through her, will occur. So without periodic rest or release of form into female, the male cannot continue to fulfill his own desire to secure form.

Likewise, the female cannot continually rest/reproduce form. She herself must sequentially effort, and does so equal to male in preparing herself to receive male as well as nurturing new form. In this fashion, she supports the securing effort of male which also secures herself. Female is actually called to surrender her life to the male desire to individualize form even though her primary desire is to unite, for without that division of the one into two there would not be the two sexual selves to unite. Conversely, at this point of unity, the male is called to surrender his life to the female desire to unite the forms even though his primary desire is to individualize. Without the unity of the two into one, there would not be a unified one from which the next division of male and female can occur.

It is important to understand the equality of the two opposite forces of male and female. They each operate under different desires and yet both are equally essential for either of them to be. The male force alone or the female force alone is impotent. Without the other neither can be. They need each other. Each is as important to the other as they are to themselves. Both are called upon to make the ultimate surrender of their lives to the other. Neither is ever without the other. Both always are. *Male and female, the two forces of creation, are what is.*

Before we proceed, just take a moment to feel your own sexuality and the sexuality of your (opposite) other half as well.

Man: Feel what it is to be a man, the man you are and will always be.
Woman: Feel what it is to be a woman, the woman you are and will always be.
Man: Feel what it is like to be a woman, the woman you are not nor will ever be.

Woman: Feel what it is like to be a man, the man you are not nor will ever be.

Now, ask yourself, what is it that you alone have to give your sexual other half and what is it you need to receive solely from your other half? From this *sexual* understanding of *our essential defining difference*, let us now know for all time:

Who am "I"?

I am a male in relationship to a female,
or
I am a female in relationship to a male
. . . whichever sexuality "I" happen to be,
"You" being the sexual opposite of me.
And they look into each other's eyes knowing for all time:

Why am "I" here?

"I" am here to express the sexuality that "I" am . . .
-Male, being that force which seeks to individualize a form separate and apart from the unity of male-female.
-Female, being that force which seeks to unite separate forms together from the division of male and female.
. . . so that together we may continue to manifest
our own sexual creation.

A man and a woman meet and a miracle occurs—a new life is formed. The miracle of life is held within their balance and love. Life, all of life, is held within their balance and love.

And finally, with this understanding of our *universal (equal but opposite) sexuality*, let us begin to behold a *living* universe of *spiritual procreation* centered on the *balance* of a man and a woman which simply is their *love* together.

The Man and Woman Relationship

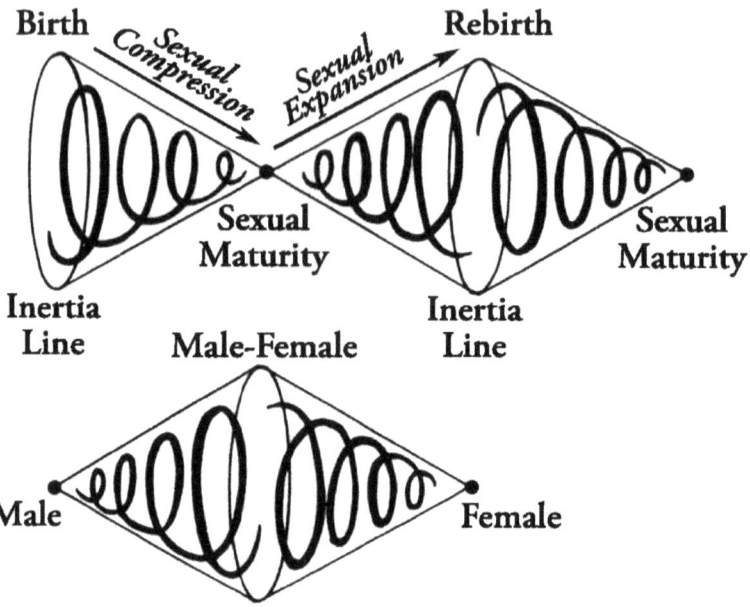

The Procreation of Life

Spiritual procreation is the center point of life. It is that place or moment when life is (pro)created, and thereby consecrated. The purpose of this writing is to bring spiritual procreation to consciousness so that each one of us may recognize that *spiritual procreation equals life*. Life is a procreation. It lies in the balanced interchange of the two equal and opposite forces of male and female. Metaphysical (sexual) balance between male and female is the key that unlocks the door to spiritual procreation in that from the balance of the two comes the next procreation of life.

Spiritual procreation is a consciousness (paradigm) shift at the metaphysical center of life. Instead of the center being a one (singular) force, i.e., "God" (or the singular individual), it is being shifted to a two equal but opposite forces, i.e., male and female. The shift is being made because a one force by itself alone is not nor can it ever be procreative to life. Spiritual procreation is that universal construct of a two forces **procreative to life**. It holds to a singular moment whereupon a man and a woman touch together in their love and, in so doing, bring forth a new moment of life. Each and every moment must be secured/reproduced through the one touch of love between a man and a woman. That one touch of love between these opposite two is the procreative center of all life.

Historically, we have not centered life on that which is procreative to life. Our concepts of "God" or spirit, etc., have been singular (inert) in their nature. *At the core spiritual level of life, we are left with something that is not procreative to life.* You might say we are left with an isolation/death rather than a *rebirth of life*. The essence of procreation (a connection or lineage) that holds us together is blocked from coming to the surface. We are unable to touch each other in (procreative) love. We need to understand that we (a man and a woman) can only unite together from our own (equal but opposite) sexual spirits. *We must know who we are sexually to unite spiritually.* We do not connect together through some intermediary. *We, male and female, unite directly through our own sexual touch.* It is we, male and female, who unite...to then divide...not something else. Spiritual procreation is only about the unity/division of a man and a woman. Why is this? Because a man and a woman *together* constitute that which is procreative to life.

When I speak of spiritual procreation, I am not speaking about some type of (mystical) procreation separate and apart from the love of a man and a woman and the birth of their child. There isn't any other type of procreation. *The complete essence of the spiritual life is the procreative touch of love between a man and a woman.* From this love—*a child is born.* This is not to suggest that each moment must somehow be a sexual embrace. Then again, maybe it does—from a heartbeat to a thought, to a glance or a whisper, to a soft touch...all in the conscious connection of a man and a woman embracing the totality of their birth-life-death-rebirth—through each other. Each moment (even physical death) can be the *only moment* where one gives his or her love to that other half. Each moment is the eternal moment of man and woman balance as the opposite two express their love for each other in everything they do. *"I love You,"* however it is expressed from a man to a woman and from a woman to a man, is as real as things can get.

Also, I am not suggesting here that every sexual embrace must result in the birth of a child. But then again, maybe I am. The procreation of life actually occurs at each (secured/reproduced) moment. When a man and a woman come together, they are actually procreating their next division—which will bring on their next union. This is equally true for elderly couples who are beyond their physical reproducing years. Their spirit together is still procreative in everything they do. The important thing to remember here is that procreation is the (spiritual) glue that permeates everything. There is a reproductive potency/fertility built into the order or structure of the universe as that order or structure. The balance/ether that permeates everything is this sex-polarized process of male and female division and unification. And then, perhaps when least expected or thought only to be a far-off hope, a man and a woman find each other and unite together in spirit, and from that union a new life begins to grow and a birth occurs and a child (male or female) is born. That new life could also be a new musical composition or some new invention, etc., but new life it is.

New life is the greatest miracle of life. And that new life is the most special life as that boy or girl grows up to take his or her place in the procreation of life—or that musical composition is played for the 1st time to an audience who feel a touch in their spirits. Everything that exists does so in some aspect or stage of the procreative process of birth-life-death-rebirth.... There just isn't any escaping the *Life Process*.

There is another term for spiritual procreation that we may use. That term is *procreative love*. Procreative love is unitive love. (Perhaps we should define unitive as a balance between the two polar opposites of division and unity.) It is where a man and a woman give their lives to each other. Notice how this giving could be quite different from what we call "sex" today. A man and a woman could be giving their lives to each other in doing the dishes or raking the leaves or holding hands and going for a walk together. Yet, another man and woman could be giving very little (and may be taking a great deal) in having sexual relations together. What we call sex without love or sex without a commitment, or even marriage, is just sex without (spiritual) giving. Promiscuity, i.e., pornography, for example, is sex without giving. It is cut off from unitive (procreative) love. Yes, one is going through the motions of the sexual act but there isn't a union of souls. One is not giving his or her **love** to the other. One is just going for his or her own gratification. The result of pornography is the deadening of one's soul. There isn't any *rebirth of spirit* to be found. Life is held in the *procreative* touch, which is a giving. It cannot be found in sexual gratification alone, which is a taking. If the sexual act is separated from unity/procreation, a death (in spirit) actually occurs. Notice the dead look in the eyes of those engaged in the pornographic industry. I mention this because today the pornographic industry is being romanticized, and thousands of men and women are entering it, or watching it, not aware of the spiritual consequences to their souls in divorcing sex from procreation. Sex cannot be separated from new creation be it the birth of a baby or the creation of spiritual touch as in art forms or new inventions. Sex lives in both thought and form—it is a union/(pro)creation of life itself. It is the vehicle of the rebirth of life, be it in thought or form, for in the birth of a baby/new creation lies our own rebirth in spirit/life. *Procreative love never separates love from sex and sex from life.*

When a man and a woman embrace in the spirit of procreative love, they touch the eternal together. I will speak more to the eternal in a later section but, for now, I want to mention that the eternal is that moment or center point that is procreative to life. Actually, the eternal is a romantic calling, not a religious one. It exists as it is procreated (moment-by-moment) out of the balance (love) of the two equal and opposite forces of male and female. We do not receive the eternal out of some belief or worship in some "higher power" but only as we give of our love to our opposite other half—**and a child is born**. I hope you can now ascertain the reality that the eternal and the procreative are one. Spiritual procreation is that (sexual) touch between a man and a woman that captures for our hearts ***"our eternal love."***

Man and Woman Forever © 1985—Selected Writings © 1991, 2010

In the beginning, male and female. Aren't 'I' either a male or else a female, just as 'You' are one or the other also? Or, more specifically, aren't 'I' a male in relation to 'You' a female, or it may be that 'I' am a female and so then 'I' am in relation to 'You' a male. Yes, 'You' and 'I' are in a sexual relationship. Whatever sexuality 'I' am, 'You' are of the opposite sexuality.

Can it be that this sexual relationship of 'You' and 'I' is true to our beings? Let us endeavor to conceive of something other. 'I' cannot. Can 'You'? I cannot conceive of my sexual self without also, at the same instance, conceiving of 'You' as that which is sexually opposite of me. All that 'I' am able to conceive of is a sexually distinct 'You' and 'I'.

Maybe it is possible to step beyond the conceptual parameter of the sexual altogether and distinguish the identities of 'You' and 'I' by another means. But how can either of us do this? We are already sexual beings. 'You' and 'I' are already sexually unique to each other. Our sexual relationship prefaces whatever we may conceptualize ourselves to be. It is impossible for either of us to conceive of ourselves without the sexual distinctions of male and female in relationship together, that is, where 'You' are of one sexuality and 'I' of the other. Our conceptual grasp begins at the sexuality of 'You' and 'I'.

In the beginning is male and female. 'I' am only as 'I' am, a sexual self of male or female, just as are 'You'. We are only sexual beings in opposite sexual manifestations. It is always 'You' and 'I' who are the manifestations of sexual being, wherever we may find ourselves to exist. Beyond this, there is nothing.

The Procreation of Life

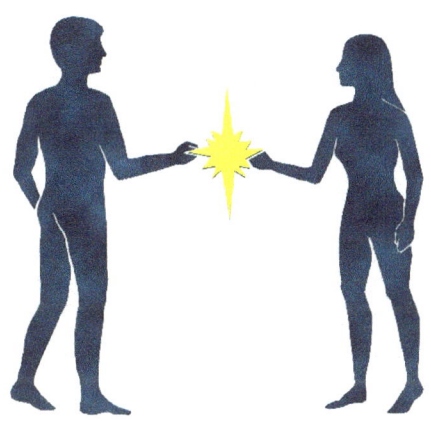

The Four Explanative Drawings of Spiritual Procreation

The four explanative drawings or models of spiritual procreation are based on the metaphysical reality of a two (equal but opposite) forces—*male and female*—that comprise life. They allow us to look at and understand any metaphysical embodiment (belief system) in the world today, or that may yet come forth, and appraise whether or not it is *procreative to life*. Simply said, we are asking, *"Is your belief system procreative to life?"* If not, it may be time to discard it for one that is. Survival is at stake.

The names I give to the drawings are generalities. Many different belief systems may cross from one model to another. My purpose here is not to appraise every belief system but to present a general overview so that you, the reader, may better understand this idea of procreative love and the importance of it centering our lives. I understand that in my analysis I might step on sensitive toes. We all hold tightly to our own beliefs. Please don't take my comments as some condemnation or personal attack upon your (eternal) soul. It is not. Nor am I suggesting that one ought not to have the right to believe (freedom of thought/worship) as one chooses. My intent here is only to illuminate those areas in our belief systems where we fail to bring in the light of procreative love and, thereby, as men and women, hinder our efforts to secure/reproduce life together.

The names I give to the four explanative drawings of spiritual procreation are: *Man and Woman Balance*, *Christianity*, *Humanism*, and *Homosexuality*. We will review each model from a procreative perspective. Each model has its own drawing as here shown and will be explained as we proceed.

The Four Explanative Drawings of Spiritual Procreation

Man and Woman Balance	Christianity	Humanism	Homosexuality
M — S — F	S	S	S
|	|	|	|
M — M — F	M — M — F	M	M
|	|	|	|
M — B — F	M — B — F	M — B — F	B

S — Spirit   M — Mind   B — Body   M — Male   F — Female

Man and Woman Balance

Man and Woman Balance is that model or structure that is procreative to life spiritually, mentally, and physically. It makes the metaphysical (sexual) distinction of a two (equal but opposite) forces on all three levels. In so doing, it presents to us the life-dynamic of a procreating universe—and a child is born.

Man and Woman Balance is the absolute of the universe. The universe is a sexual us, i.e., male and female. Together (dividing and uniting...), **and only together**, are we procreative to life. Our life together is held in the balance we comprise. Equal and opposite is the structure that defines (the limits of) balance, i.e., procreation. Upon this structural balance of male and female all life rests.

Structural Balance

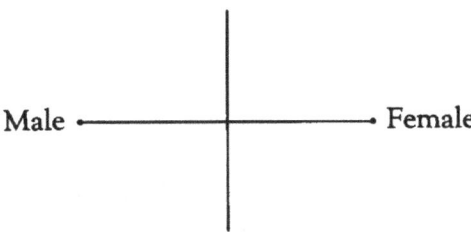

Man and Woman Balance as a (procreative) metaphysic arises out of the discovery/distinction of two forces. In this discovery of two sexual forces lies the paradigm shift from a one force ("God")

to the two forces of male and female. In the two forces lies the balance (equal but opposite) which gives to us procreative understanding. Another word for balance is sovereigncy.* We could say man and woman sovereigncy. In the structural balance of male and female, each man <u>and</u> woman are sovereign. Sovereigncy does not come from a (one-force) "God" but from our (male and female) balance together. Nothing, not "God," nor the state, nor the King or Pope etc., is sovereign over us. Do you understand that your life sovereigncy lies in the balance you metaphysically hold with your equal but opposite other half?

*I am using the term sovereigncy (rather than sovereignty) to connote our co-sovereignty or interdependence together. Sovereignty only lies in the balance of the <u>two</u> equal and opposite forces.

Historically, we have been encased in the one-force paradigm. As such, the balance of male and female was hidden from view. It was hidden behind the veil of "one force" which, by its very nature, distorts the balance. A "singular force" does not allow for the balance of the two forces. We are left with having to choose one side over the other as the (more important) "singular" force. At that moment, the balance of male and female becomes imbalanced. The chosen side is viewed as "superior" and the other side "inferior." This superior/inferior structure is known as hierarchy. Instead of co-sovereignty, we have some form of master/slave scenario in play. Man and woman imbalance is always structured in some one-force belief of superior/inferior. We may believe that our own race or sex is greater than another's or that we are lesser than "God" or the state. In any event, the outcome is an imbalance between oneself and one's opposite other half. Imbalance affects or distorts the inherent spiritual connection between the sexual two and procreative love (which is also spiritual love) is thereby denied.

This sexual imbalance of superior/inferior shows itself in one of two ways. These two ways are known as masculinism and feminism. Masculinism is that (imbalanced) model or structure that holds men as metaphysically superior to women. "Thank God I am a man," is the thought held by these men. Masculinism holds to the difference (opposition) between men and women but not their equality (equal necessity). Its structure then is opposite but not equal, and because of this imbalance it blocks a man and a woman from uniting together (in spirit) in procreative love. The cardinal sin of every man in any one-force masculinist structure is that he fails to acknowledge and choose woman as his life's completion (salvation). The common saying of women, "Men just don't get it," has much truth to it. What men don't get is woman: primarily, his existent need for her. How can he if he is embedded in some one-force hierarchical structure where he is called to worship some "higher power" (which just may be himself) rather than give his love (security) to his equal but opposite other half? The damage, the heartache, the pain, hostility, and brutality that men have heaped upon women down through the ages, just so he could cling to the mis-premise of his own superiority, is staggering. And it is still going on right now at this moment the world over. Men don't get it. They really don't understand the absolute necessity of spiritual union with a woman. As such they are not able to touch her at her deepest placement—her procreative soul (womb). And all of the sexual techniques in the world will not help him for his spirit has not acknowledged her essential nature and necessity in his life. That is his sin.

    Feminism is that (imbalanced) model or structure that holds women as metaphysically superior to men. "I don't need any man," is the thought behind these women. The feminist model is just the reverse of the masculinist model. The feminist holds to the equality of the two sexes but not their essential difference or opposition. In a way, this is understandable. Women have had their sex (sexual difference) used against them for so long that they are suspect of any claim or classification of them based on their sex. Many women have a deep distrust of men and even a rage in their souls. They, women, have been hurt. But that fact alone ought not justify the implementation of an imbalanced structure that is not true to the interdependent reality of man and woman. We, men and women, are equal to and opposite from one another. That is our primordial relationship upon which all life rests. The feminist model of equal but not opposite equally blocks the spiritual touch of procreative life. Whereas a masculinist man cannot touch the soul of woman, a feminist woman cannot allow a man to truly touch her deepest soul. She will not want to let him into her heart, at least not all the way, and that is her sin. Letting a man all the way in would constitute her surrender, the feminist's greatest fear. Both the masculinist and the feminist cannot give their lives to each other. Their spiritual imbalance blocks the one touch of procreative love. As such, both of these models much be rejected.

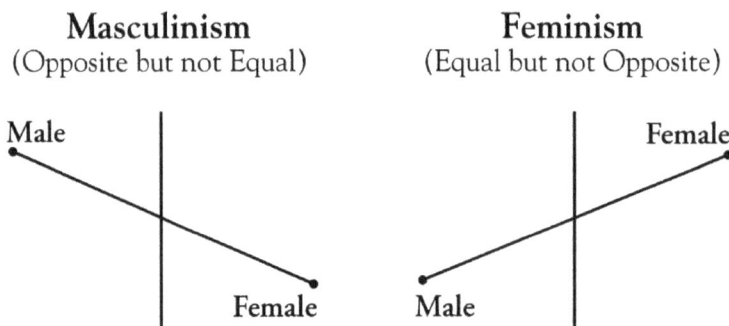

Structural Imbalance

Masculinism (Opposite but not Equal) — Male / Female

Feminism (Equal but not Opposite) — Female / Male

All one-force models will reveal themselves to be (spiritually) imbalanced on either the male side or the female side. Only Man and Woman Balance, with its procreative structure of equal and opposite, holds both sexes in the absolute sovereigncy (specialness and sacredness) that they each comprise. Life is a together enterprise. The quantum universe (of all life) is framed in an "us," not a "me." (It doesn't exclude "me," it just includes "you.") The "us" of life is a "sexual us," male and female. Without this "sexual us"—in balance—life cannot be. There isn't any life dynamic in masculinism or feminism. Balance, and thus procreation, exists only in the context of equal and opposite. All balance—by definition—is Man and Woman Balance. Man and Woman Balance is the procreative dynamic of the whole of this *universe of life*.

Christianity* is that model or structure that does not make the two-force (sexual/procreative distinction) of equal and opposite on the spiritual (metaphysical) level. In other words, spiritually speaking, Christianity is not sexual, i.e., procreative to life. It is a one-force creationist (first creator) model that, I might add, generally includes all religions past and present. In Christianity, and other religions, the two equal but opposite forces of male and female are not to be found at the center point of creation itself and thus the essential procreative balance of life is obstructed.

*We essentially could include any religion is this model but, in this writing, I am focusing on Christianity as that is the religion of my upbringing.

Man and Woman Balance

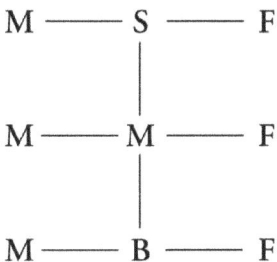

Christianity

In Christianity, sexuality (the two forces of male and female) is acknowledged physically and, even to some degree, mentally. Most Christians understand what it means to say that men and women are purposively different or that it takes a man and a woman to make a baby. They just don't equate or connect this spiritually. They have yet to *universalize* the procreative process and thereby understand that even "God" does not and cannot exist outside of or separate from procreation, i.e., male and female. As a result, in this (one-force) model, we are left with a spiritual imbalance between male and female. This is evidenced by the male-oriented Trinity (God the Father, God the Son, and God the Holy Spirit) and the Virgin Birth which claims holy union separate from the union of a man and a woman.

In the model of Man and Woman Balance, we understand "God" to be representative of the (holy) procreative balance of the two forces. We would say that there is both a Father God and a Mother God, both equal in necessity but opposite in purpose. Or we could say that "God," i.e., *procreative balance* is only expressed in the one (eternal) touch of love between a man and a woman. That touch (or union) is a holy touch. The spiritual union and marriage of a man and a woman and the birth of their child is as holy as things get. Every union between a man and a woman is the *most blessed union* and every child born is *a Christ child*. Jesus doesn't have a monopoly on being the Christ as the church suggests. We are all invited. As the 12th century Christian mystic Meister Eckhart (1260–1327) stated: *"Every son is the only begotten son."* True as this statement is, it is not fully balanced. We must also proclaim: *Every daughter is the only begotten daughter.* Every son and every daughter are a Christ son or a Christ daughter born from the holy union of a man and a woman. But due to the Trinity and Virgin Birth, we, man and woman, are excluded from holy union with each other. We are told there is a more "Godly" union, one that we cannot quite get to by ourselves alone—that only through Jesus can we find salvation, or so it is believed. Perhaps we all should take a vow of chastity and commit our lives to the church, if only to get a wee bit closer to that holy union. But this misses the point, does it not? Spiritual union itself is sexual in its nature. This is to say, it lies in the procreative balance of the two equal but opposite forces of male and female. In other words, *we can only unite in spirit with our equal but opposite other half.* That union is a *procreative touch* and is the most holy of unions.

In the one-force (hierarchical) consciousness perhaps we do need the Christ imagery to define and experience holiness. Certainly, the Trinity and Virgin Birth are a part of that imagery. But this model cannot bring us into a direct and complete spiritual touch (holiness) with our equal but opposite other half. Spiritual procreation is a direct touch between a man and a woman. There isn't any intermediary to go through. There is only one man and one woman touching in their love together. And in that one most precious moment—a child is born. Do you see this? The Trinity is actually the division/unification (procreative) process between a male and a female. The Trinity must be procreative to life or it fails.

The Holy Trinity

Male-Female

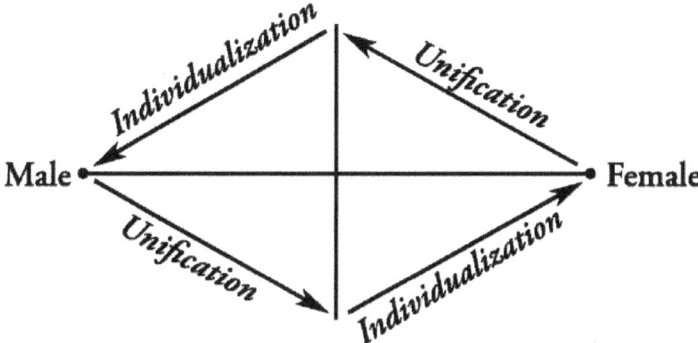

Religion, as we know it, is a one-force (hierarchical) imbalance between man (a man or a woman) and "God." It is this imbalance that kills our souls. This imbalance has been given the name *original sin*. Original sin supposedly was due to the disobedience of Adam and Eve in the Garden of Eden. Indeed, Adam and Eve may have turned away from "God" (spiritual union), but the original sin was structured in the metaphysical imbalance from the start. It exists in any hierarchical structure (superior/inferior). The whole belief/worship paradigm of religion is hierarchical and leaves us all in sin (imbalance). From this sin or imbalance, we are unable to spiritually unite with our equal but opposite other half. Spiritual union, i.e., procreation cannot occur in a hierarchical relationship. The parts must be balanced. Religious hierarchy gives to us self-righteousness, spiritual bondage, the worship of oneself, the lust for power and control, the denial of a pure sexual touch, the denial of sovereigncy and unalienable rights, ending in envy, poverty, physical aggression, and war. Spiritual balance (between the two forces) gives to us eternal love. Take your pick.

Hierarchy as to Balance

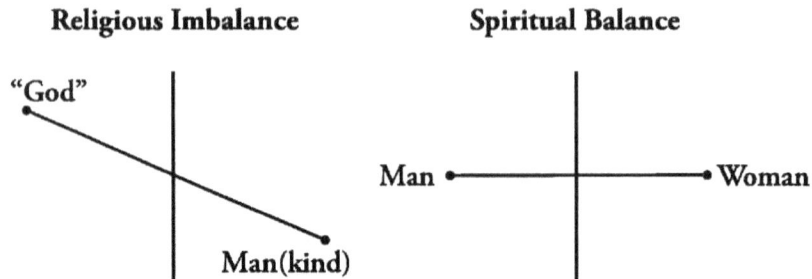

The message of Jesus can be viewed in one of two ways. From a one-force or hierarchical perspective, Jesus is the only son of "God," born of a Virgin, who died on a Cross for our sins, and was resurrected for our eternal life. In essence, the hierarchical message of Jesus is that he alone is Christ/saviour. The Bible tells us that the Jews rejected Jesus as saviour—that perhaps the Jews were looking for a saviour to confirm/implement their own perceived status as the "chosen people." But maybe Jesus wasn't about hierarchy (a singular Christ or chosen people) at all. Maybe his real message—and threat—was that the Christ lay within us all as love and that in love no one is to be excluded nor was anyone to be considered (metaphysically) superior or inferior to another. His message was not about the righteousness of this belief over that belief but rather was, and still is, a *message of love*. The miracle of his life is that he, born a man, rose to the spiritual level of eternal love. He never asked to be our saviour per se for the original sin/salvation scenario did not exist for him. That only exists in the world of hierarchical imbalance. Once the two parts of the (man and woman) relationship are balanced, spiritual or divine love shines through. It is really an insult to his spirit that we ask him to "save" us. After all, he needs our love as much as we need his! We all need to give and receive love; that is the *balance.* That is the spiritual touch or procreation of life. The message of spiritual procreation actually completes the message of Jesus in that it slays the dragon of hierarchical imbalance once and for all and leaves us only with our equal but opposite other half in the divine presence of our *procreative love.*

We must understand that Christianity, or any religion, cannot take us to the eternal. Religions speak of transcendence—from individual separateness to a unification or universality of our souls. But that is only one half of the procreative process. From unity comes the next division (rebirth) into sexed individuality. The eternal is not some singular transcendent state. It is a sexual, i.e., procreative process between the two forces of male and female that includes both transcendence (unity) and, what I call, *incendence* (division). The eternal is the whole birth-life-death--rebirth...sexual (life) dynamic that exists only in the *now* as an act of (procreative) love between a man and a woman. The eternal can only be found in **Man and Woman Balance**, i.e., *spiritual procreation*.

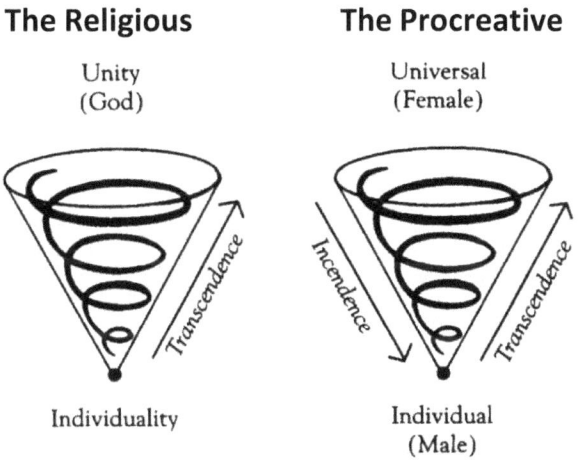

Let me take a moment and comment on what is called Eastern thought or Eastern religion. There are a number of people who consider Eastern thought more profound and less dogmatic than Christianity. In Eastern thought, the focus is on the universal or eternal self. When we hear the words "I Am" (words Jesus also uttered), the meaning here is not in reference to one's individual or physical self but to one's universal or spiritual self. The quest, as I understand it, is to transcend the individual self to this universal I Am. This universal self, supposedly, is the real self and lies deep within each one of us. It is found beyond the chattering of the mind or the world of motion and appearance. "Be still and know that thou art God," it is said. In this stillness (supposedly) lies a pure experience or consciousness of the Eternal Self, a being-ness or oneness without attributes or definition. In Eastern thought, we might say that our "true self" does not need salvation for it is already eternal.

Having said all this I must ask, is this "pure consciousness" or "being-ness" procreative to life? In other words, can one, as "eternal Self," by oneself alone, make a baby? You see, the "eternal Self" of Eastern thought is still singular. The two-force sexual process of birth-life-death-rebirth... is nowhere to be found. As such, that will not work. The focus of life must be on that exact sexual, procreative man and woman process/interaction that itself comprises life. Stillness (even if we define stillness to be the unity point of the division of man and woman) is not by itself the source or center point of life. The source or center point of life includes *both* the unification of the equal and opposite two and the division of the united one. In speaking of stillness, it does not come without motion, both equal to but opposite from each other and both *real. Everything has its opposite.* Stillness is not more important (superior to) than motion. Pure consciousness is not more important than individual expression. Being-ness is not more important than separate appearance. These things exist as parts of a relationship together—equal and opposite. *One is not without the other; both are needed for either to be.* Do you understand this? *There isn't a singular point of cause or source*. This abstraction is crucial. It is the abstraction between a one order and a *two forces*. Let us take the mystery out of Eastern thought and see it for what it is—*unsexed*. Maybe I am somewhat old-fashioned—I just happen to believe/experience that holding your (and your spouses') baby in your arms is about as real (and eternal) as things can get for you. Isn't that a moment of "pure consciousness"?

Perhaps we ought to be grateful for what Christianity and Eastern thought have given to us—the markings of relationship and eternal life. In the one-force paradigm that was the best we could do. But I want a complete touch with my other half as my present moment/eternal experience right now. I hope you do as well. Our salvation lies in our sexual (procreative) balance *together*. There isn't any singular salvation or eternal life. Our eternal life can only be found in our *balance together*. Let us, as men and women, reach out to each other in our (securitive or reproductive) love right now and *touch*—and a child is born.

Now, in defense of Christianity, I will state, it certainly is a better system than what follows, Humanism and Homosexuality. Unfortunately, Christianity will never be able to defend itself against the onslaught of either as we shall see.

Christianity

```
          S
          |
  M ————— M ————— F
          |
  M ————— B ————— F
```

Humanism

Humanism is that model or structure where the two (procreative) forces are denied on both the spiritual and mental levels. The necessity (difference) of a man and a woman together is accepted physically but not mentally or spiritually. Can you see the separation occurring here? In our discussion of Christianity, the connection between man and woman was spiritually aborted. In Humanism, it is mentally aborted as well. Our hearts and minds become disconnected from each other.

The Humanist (who can also be called the Socialist) generally rejects the "other worldliness" of religion. The Humanist man or woman looks to this world for his or her (material) salvation through the state (Leviathan). The state, or *nation-state* as I often refer to it, rather than "God," is the supreme or sovereign entity of life. (It's still a one-force hierarchy but under a different name.) Instead of "God" being the master and the individual the servant, the state or government is now the master and the individual the slave. The Humanist model includes most if not all socio/political forms of government in the world today including Marxism/communism, socialism (communism by vote), nationalistic, religious, or racial fascism, corporate (fascist) capitalism, welfare democracy, and special (group) rights egalitarianism. We see a good example of Humanism in the feminist movement today where women claim (mental) equality to men, (women were never unequal, just different), even claiming they don't necessarily/existentially need a man and yet, at the same time, turning to the state for their protection and welfare. Well, if you think men are bad, wait until you meet his fascist master. Perhaps George Orwell (1903–1950), in his book *1984*, said it best: *"If you want a picture of the future, imagine a boot stomping on a human face—forever."* That boot is Humanism.

The first thing to understand about Humanism is that all "rights" originate from the state. This is the Humanist doctrine or creed. These rights are called "human rights" or "civil rights" or some such name. Whatever they are called, they stand inside the nation-state. The state is superior to them—to you and me. At one time, at least in the experiment in freedom called America, there was the idea that rights originate outside of or prior to the state. These rights were called *unalienable rights* because they could not be liened (encumbered or taken away). They acknowledged and positioned the individual prior to the state. We don't hear much about unalienable rights anymore even though they were the cornerstone of all the freedoms that once existed in America. If we did, we would know or learn that unalienable rights are those claims or guarantees given to us not by the state but by the very nature of life itself and the *survival requirement* placed upon each one of us. Every one of us must consume to live. And to consume, we must **produce**. That basis of our life survival lies in two fundamental/unalienable rights: **Liberty**—*the right for one to act or effort as to one's choosing* and **Justice**—*the right (or obligation) for one to receive the consequences of one's actions.* I call these two rights the unalienable rights of *earning* and *owning*, the fundamental rights of the sovereign life that exists prior to any form of government.

The founding fathers of America recognized these unalienable rights calling them *self-evident* and *God-given*. This meant that these rights were prior to government. This conception of unalienable rights was a tremendous illumination on the pathway to freedom. Unfortunately, the concept of "God" was still stuck in its own one-force imbalance (hierarchy) and these rights were not held absolutely or inclusively, chattel slavery being one obvious example. Hierarchy (mater/slave) still ruled man's mind. Not until we understand the metaphysical balance of man and woman (and their absolute *sovereigncy*) will we be able to slay the hierarchical dragon of the master/slave imbalance and bring unalienable rights to all. *Not greater than, not lesser than, we, you and I, are sovereign.*

The Nation-State **Man and Woman Balance**

Master/Slave Sovereigncy
(Civil Rights) (Unalienable Rights)

Government

Man — Woman

Individual

The Unalienable Rights of Man and Woman

- *The Right to Earn.*
- *The Right to Own (what one earns).*

The Unalienable Rights Test

- *A right must be based in individual life.*
- *A right must be the same for everyone.*
- *A right can never be taken away.*
- *A right cannot be a (consumptive) need.*
- *A right can never circumvent the choice (right) of another.*

The intention of the Humanist is to control the means of production for his or her own consumption. What this means is the control of the economy, i.e., your and my pocketbooks. This is the Humanist sole intention and effort. Whether the system is fascist, communist, or "democratic," it does not matter. What does matter is that you pay up. Democracy is actually the most effective Humanist system as it gives the appearance of some freedom with "elected government." What a democracy really consists of is a system where all people are equally liable for the governmental debt. (See the 14th Amendment to the United States Constitution.) In America, we hear about the "good faith and credit of the American people." What credit? Is someone promising and pledging our future earnings to someone else? Is the politician's promise our perpetual debt? Chattel slavery, where one person owns another, was one of the reasons for the Civil War.* Hopefully, chattel slavery has been abolished. But chattel slavery isn't the only slavery. There is also economic (tax) slavery. Economic slavery is known as peonage. According to Black's Law Dictionary, peonage is a condition of servitude compelling a person to perform labor in order to pay off a debt. What if the debt is not due to your or my individual actions (which would be our own individual responsibility) but is a collective debt placed upon all people by the ruling elites? Would not a collective debt be the best way to keep us in economic bondage—if that was the intention—without our even knowing about it?

*Perhaps the "unintended" consequence of the Civil War was the 14th Amendment to the Constitution which created a new class of citizen— the federal citizen (peon) under the jurisdiction of the federal government. We are all slaves now.

The idea of a government controlling a people through debt is not new. Governments historically have attempted to control the money system. When Jesus said, *"Give to Caesar what is Caesar's"* he was referring to a Roman coin with Caesar's mark or stamp on it. Was not that Caesar's coin? Is not all government script the government's property? For our purposes, I want to begin my analysis in 1848 with the publication of *The Communist Manifesto* written by Karl Marx and Fredrick Engels. The ten planks of the

Manifesto basically describe the way to take over any economy. Implement these ten planks and you control everyone's wallet. Remember, I said the sole purpose of the Humanist was to control your pocketbook. *The Communist Manifesto* is the Humanist Bible, although few would publicly admit that today. Let's review the ten planks of the manifesto and its closing statement.

1. Abolition of property in land and application of all rents of land to public purposes.
2. A heavy progressive or graduated income tax.
3. Abolition of all rights of inheritance.
4. Confiscation of the property of all emigrants and rebels.
5. Centralization of credit in the hands of the State, by means of a national bank with State capital and an exclusive monopoly.
6. Centralization of the means of communication and transport in the hands of the State.
7. Extension of factories and instruments of production owned by the State, and bringing into cultivation of waste lands, and the improvement of the soil generally in accordance with a common plan.
8. Equal liability of all to labor. Establishment of industrial armies, especially for agriculture.
9. Combination of agriculture with manufacturing industries; gradual abolition of the distinction between town and country by a more equable distribution of population over the country.
10. Free education for all children in public schools. Abolition of children's factory labor in its present form. Combination of education with industrial production.

"When, in the course of development, class distinctions have disappeared, and all production has been concentrated in their hands of a vast association of the whole nation, the public power will lose its political character."

Some of the wording in the Manifesto is dated, but it should not surprise you to learn that most if not all of these ten planks have been implemented in some form or another into the American system. Contrast this to the immortal words of Thomas Jefferson in *The Declaration of Independence* of 1776: *"We hold these truths to be self-evident, that all men are created equal, that they are endowed by their Creator with certain unalienable Rights, that among these are Life, Liberty and the pursuit of Happiness."* In this one sentence stands the whole spirit and freedom of the American dream and yet, instead of *The Declaration of Independence* and its corresponding unalienable rights being cherished, we have the unrelenting onslaught of the ten planks of *The Communist Manifesto.* How can this be? When was this done, by whom, and why did not we hear about it?

The economic takeover of the United States of America began on the day America was formed. A battle between Jefferson and Alexander Hamilton was being fought over the issue of a central bank. What is a central bank and why is this concern important? Essentially, the purpose of a central bank is to control the money system of a country. Control the money and you can control the economy. Andrew Jackson, the 7th President of the United States, risked his whole presidency on slaying the central bank that had been formed. In 1913, the central bank was resurrected under the name Federal Reserve System.* The FED, as it is called, was created to control the money system of the United States—the 5th plank of *The Communist Manifesto*—not for the PEOPLE but for the banksters/politicians themselves. The FED actually is not federal; it is privately owned, but both it and the government need each other to carry out the Humanist plan.

* See *The Secret of the Federal Reserve*—Eustace Mullins, 1991**

**Author's note: Some of Eustace Mullins writings have been criticized as being anti-Semitic. Well, I, too, do not subscribe to the Jewish (chosen people) theory of history as, I believe, the Light lies within us all. So let us not be so hasty in dismissing Mullin's thorough research on the Federal Reserve System. Imagine the courage to even write such a book.

The Federal Reserve Note (FRN) was created to replace the United States of America *dollar*. The dollar actually represented a *substance value*. It represented a certain standard weight of a commodity—gold or silver. The key to the value of the dollar, or of any paper money certificate, lies in its redemption to the actual thing (gold or silver) it represents. The first FRNs were also redeemable. You could take them to a bank and exchange them for their declared worth (weight) in gold or silver. Redemption is the great check on any group or government taking over an economy through a money system. They themselves would have to make good for the actual value of the money they were issuing. They could not create/place a bondage of debt on the people.

In 1933, the United States government was declared bankrupt. Then President Franklin D. Roosevelt, through Executive Order, on March 9, 1933, signed the Emergency Banking Relief Act. (The bankruptcy was confirmed by Congress under House Joint Resolution 192 on June 5, 1933.) From that moment on, the United States has been insolvent. It is the debtor of a Chapter 11 bankruptcy. (Remember the statement "the good faith and credit of the American people"? We, you and I, are now the debtor.) Now, the question we need to ask ourselves is: *Who is the creditor?* On April 5, 1933, through another Executive Order, President Roosevelt began calling in the gold of the American people. It actually became illegal to own gold! The gold went to the FED but, more importantly, it broke the link between the FRN and gold. By law, FRNs were no longer redeemable in gold. The monetary takeover was complete. From that day on, the United States of America, its Constitution with its corresponding unalienable rights and its gold-backed dollar, ceased to exist. In its place was put the Federal Reserve System, the Federal Reserve Note, the Internal Revenue System, and taxpayer or debtor status upon us all.

Now, take a moment and pull out a "dollar bill" from your wallet. It still says "One Dollar" but that no longer signifies a weight but a number. It also says "FEDERAL RESERVE NOTE." What is a Federal Reserve Note? Who holds title to it? What is its interest rate? When is it due? What does it mean when it says, "THIS NOTE IS LEGAL TENDER FOR ALL DEBTS, PUBLIC AND PRIVATE"? What debt? My question is, how can a note serve as a currency or money for a people? A note signifies an indebtedness. What debt? Is it the government's debt that is being placed upon the American people? But it is much more sinister than that. The FED creates FRNs out of credit demand. (The welfare state demands "something-for-nothing" money.) The FRN actually is a loan to the government—or to you and I. The loan is to be paid back, with interest of course. In essence, the FED is the creditor and you and I are the debtor. This creditor/debtor relationship is created at that precise moment a FRN is printed. *FRNs equal our debt.* Debt is our (economic) bondage. *Do you understand that structured into any credit/debit system of money creation is debt bondage for the people using that "money"?*

Now let us understand that the FRN is created as a credit. It is not an organically earned substance-value as is gold or silver. Someone has a "legal" monopoly to print paper money and sell it as legal tender. But because it is not real substance-value it automatically creates a continuous pressure on prices for goods and services. In a credit/debit system, prices will always rise. We continue to get less for the money. In other words, we work harder for less and less. Sound familiar? Can't even make it on a two-income household anymore. The FRN is actually phony (monopoly) money, also called counterfeit money. How would you like to have a monopoly to print paper money such that people would have to accept it and use it—and pay it back to you plus interest? What a scam. But don't tell anyone you know about it. This is the exact thing we can't talk about. Nobody mentions it, do they? The Federal Reserve System is the greatest fraud in history and nobody wants to talk about it. You can be sure the politicians won't speak of it—they are in on it!

Let's ask another question, what is the purpose/necessity of the Internal Revenue Service (IRS)? "Collect taxes," you say? But why would taxes need to be collected if the FED can print all the money it wants? The purpose and necessity of the IRS is two-fold. One is to give to the FRN the appearance of value through demand. If the FED just printed all the money it wanted, its money would be worthless—as it truly is. It would inflate to zero value and the counterfeit money scheme would be exposed. But if you place a tax on "income" (actually defined as corporate profit or the wages of government employees) you decrease the potential for value creation/ownership and, at the same time, you increase government control over your life and property. Any credit/debit system needs an (income) tax component. Notice that the IRS was created at the same time the FED was created, in 1913. Also note that the income tax is the 2nd plank of *The Communist Manifesto* but was explicitly rejected by the Founding Fathers of the United States of America.

It may be safe to say that the hidden but perhaps most important purpose of the IRS is control. You might say that their primary task is to see that all Americans (U.S. citizens we are called) are enrolled in the FED credit/debit system. Enrollment in this system identifies you as a debtor slave. You are called a "taxpayer." You file an "Income Tax Return." You have an "identification number" such as a Social Security Number. You even have an all Capital letters name which is not your true birth name but your corporate or commercial name that identifies you as a "human resource," collateral for the debt. You see, you are not a sovereign American with unalienable rights anymore but a U.S. resident/citizen with civil (debtor) "rights." You can't own money, only use debt notes at a cost. You can't even own property today. You lease what you think is your home for a cost or tax. If you don't pay the tax, you forfeit the property, so *whose property is it?* It just goes on and on. To get a job you must fill out a "wage form." To open a business, you must get a "license." To get married you must also get a "license," and to have a child you need a "Birth Certificate" with a "Social Security Number." You are signed up before you even open your eyes! Even to vote, that great heritage of a freeman, you must signify that you are a "U.S. citizen." Such is life in the counterfeit credit/debit money matrix. You own nothing. It has already been stolen from you. Do you understand?

What has occurred in the United States of America with the takeover of the monetary system is now happening world-wide. With the creation of the International Monetary Fund (IMF)/World Bank (WB) after World War II, this credit-from-nothing scheme has gone global. The IMF/WB issues (from nothing) to each country Special Drawing Rights (SDRs) that are monetary credits. The people of those countries are obliged to pay the credit back with interest. In just a few short years, almost every country on earth is millions if not billions (or trillions) of dollars (or pounds, franks, yens, etc.) in debt. Now you have to ask yourself, where did the IMF/WB get all this money (credit) to loan? They created it out of nothing. And it is our ever-growing debt. This global credit/debit scheme is what is known as the One-World Order. It is a one-world order of debt bondage where our every economic decision is tracked by government agencies (FinCEN, NSA, Interpol, IRS, etc.) and "money hoarding" becomes the universal crime of anyone who seeks anonymity in their *private* financial affairs. Perhaps in the not-so-distant future we will all be "United Nations citizens" with all those special "human rights" as we slave together to pay off an ever-increasing global debt. It is this debt that is destroying this planet. It rips not just at our economic fabric where families cannot make it anymore but at our moral fabric as well where the future of a generation is mortgaged away—their souls stolen—and we wonder why our kids just can't sit still! We must understand that money is a *value*. It cannot be created from nothing. It is formed out of idea and effort. Until money is free, i.e., a free-market commodity, owned by the individual who has created/earned a value, we will never be free. And not one politician, judge, legislator, lawyer, banker, bureaucrat, educator...Humanist wants that to happen. Remember, the Humanist has only one thing in mind—to control your pocketbook.

The Constitution of the Universe

- *Each individual life is sovereign.*
- *Every individual has the unalienable right to earn as he or she chooses and to keep what he or she earns.*
- *No individual, group, or government shall initiate force, or threat of, against another individual.*
- *And so it is given.*

Humanism*

```
        S
        |
        |
        M
        |
        |
M ——— B ——— F
```

*Has anyone noticed that the size of government is inversely proportional to the freedom (wealth and health) of the people to which it claims it is here to serve!

Homosexuality

Homosexuality is that structure or model that does not make the two-force sexual distinction on the spiritual, mental, or physical levels. By definition, it excludes one half of the universe (the gay male excludes female and the lesbian female excludes male) and, as a result, is not procreative to life. I understand that many accept and even demand a person's right to choose their own "way of life." So do I. But I think it is also important to understand that homosexuality is not a "way of life." You see, *it takes a man and a woman to make a baby*. That really is all we should have to say on that matter. Yet the homosexual seeks to legitimize homosexuality placing it on an "equal par" or as an "equal alternative" to the union between a man and a woman (forgetting that two men cannot unite the two and two women cannot divide the one). The homosexual quest is not just to have a choice but to have that choice accepted as a "life equivalent" to a *man, woman, and child* and thereby be incorporated into all aspects of society. But it isn't equivalent because it is not procreative. Don't we understand this?

Historically, the sexual act was viewed as that union between one man and one woman that brought forth a new life. Sex and procreation were one and the same. This *procreative union* was an expression of love. What we call *unitive love* was (and is) procreative love. It was understood that when a man and woman unite (in spirit) the *two become as one*. And from that *one* the next division of life (a birth) can occur. Two men can't become "as one." (The bolt must go into the nut.) With two women it is just the opposite; they can't divide. In both cases that *touch of procreation* cannot occur. Whatever homosexuality is, it is not comprised of sexual union (marriage), and it is not capable of bringing forth the birth of a child (family). Yet today, homosexuality is being promoted as if it is some spiritual/sexual liberation. It is the exact opposite actually. Rather than a birth of life, we have a death of life. But don't tell anyone. To speak this is considered to be a "spiritual assault" on the homosexual's very psyche. There are already laws in place which make what I am saying a "hate crime" against the homosexual. Now, let us think this through. Are we to say that it is to be a "hate crime" to suggest that it takes a man and a woman to make a baby—or that the sanctity of life actually is embedded in the birth of life? Is this what we have come to?

I understand that the homosexual person would claim that that is just how he or she is. Call it genetic or biological or how one feels inside (in spirit), certainly we should not reject another for that, should we? Fine, but don't call it a marriage or don't seek to have children (adoption, surrogate/IVF etc.). That crosses the line into the procreative which is what the homosexual has already rejected. That is what the homosexual does not want to admit which is why such people seek the legal right to marry and have children in some fashion as if some external law will legitimize an unnatural act. To admit that they are rejecting procreation exposes their whole game as being anti-life. And that is exactly what it is. The question we should be asking ourselves is not why someone is "homosexual" but why one is rejecting procreation/life.

There may be many reasons why one has homosexual impulses. We all tend to deny the true spiritual/procreative connection when we have been hurt, a hurt/wound which fundamentally is always due to a disconnection from the eternal, i.e., procreative love. Sometimes our pain is so great inside that we don't or can't look at it. The reason is because underneath it all is our greatest fear—*nothingness*. That is right. Our greatest fear is that if we really look within ourselves we will find nothing, the void of our own *spiritual extinction*. Might the homosexual simply be one who has not faced his or her own extinction? Well, they are not alone. Neither has the Christian (on the spiritual level) or the Humanist (on the spiritual and mental level). All of these things are nothing more than attempts to cover up that "existential nothingness" that lies in their souls. But why does that "nothingness" lie in the center of one's soul? Because one has not understood the procreative necessity that is life. None of us make it in life without the procreative nexus. The procreative is our nexus to the eternal. We can only get to the eternal through our *equal and opposite* other half, not through Jesus or the nation-state or the same sex. When will we learn?

There is great controversy today over what has been called reparative therapy that claims to "cure" a person of his or her homosexual desires. Actually, the issue is not that complex when we understand that homosexuality is a metaphysical imbalance. The "cure" is the same as the cure for Christianity and Humanism; one must understand that there are two equal and opposite forces to the universe. It is only in the balance of man and woman that we are able to *touch in spirit* which causes the "nothingness" to disappear. So, whoever you are, whatever your specific situation is, lift that illusion of imbalance from your soul by saying *The Eternal Prayer*. *The Eternal Prayer* is just our own prayer to our own eternal (equal and opposite) other half. In so saying this prayer, all metaphysical imbalances forever disappear.

The Eternal Prayer

My blessed love, please come into my heart and live in me. Allow me, as well, to come into your heart and live in you. Let us, from this moment on, live in each other's hearts, our love together being our guide, shining a light for all to see that life is held simply in our balance together.

A related topic that I think we need to discuss is abortion. Irrespective of what the law is on abortion, and I would have disagreements with the findings of Roe v. Wade that made abortion legal under the concept of a woman's right to choose/privacy, we must ask ourselves, how have we come to the killings of babies? I would submit to you that the abortion has already occurred between the man and the woman in a "sexual embrace" that did not unite their spirits together, and the effect of that disconnection is abortion, the eventual killing of the baby. You see, if a man and woman are not connecting in love than a disconnection is occurring. That man and woman are not spiritually uniting. They have not bonded in love prior to the sexual encounter. Yes, they are having sex, but their spirits are not uniting together. If they were, abortion would be out of the question. A man and a woman who understand the significance of life in its holy and sacred nature are not about to kill it. So why are not the man and woman uniting in spirit? The primary reason is that they are not holding to a spirit of balance/procreation. Again, it is a metaphysical issue. What the man and the woman bring to their "union" is what they get. If they are bringing to their relationship an imbalance (either in the form of masculinism or feminism), that will show in their "union." In fact, they will not fully unite and to the degree they do not unite, there is an "abortion of spirit." A separation will occur between them and everything they do. That imbalance will surface in the form of abortion or in other things like divorce or adultery. If they do have children, that imbalance will show up as part of the structural/neurological make-up of their children. There isn't any escaping anything we do. The cause/effect, i.e., balance of the universe is exact. It is all based on procreative love. The solution to the abortion issue is loving man and woman relationships.

Now, let us take this a step further and ask ourselves, what is premarital sex? Is it not sex guaranteed to create an abortion on the spiritual level, not to mention the physical level? Hey, I don't want to sound like a prude here; there are lots of things a couple can do as they get to know and love each other. Certainly, starting at 1st base rather than 3rd base (or even home plate) would be warranted. In a truly balanced *committed* marriage, the sexual embrace comes after the marriage vow. Marriage is a (procreative) commitment. *Its consummation must come after the (marriage) commitment.* We can't have a union of souls in premarital sex. As such, premarital sex is a form of abortion. The abortion of life is its consequence. We want to have our sex without consequence and life just doesn't work that way. Everything has a consequence. We might say that the sexual embrace itself, its eternal balance, is the center point of consequence. If you engage in sex without thought as to what you are bringing to it, such as a real-life commitment in marriage or the birth of child, you will pay the price of that imbalance. If I had to find one mis-premise that has opened Pandora's (sexual) box leading to abortion, adultery, divorce, and even homosexuality, I would cite premarital sex. Sex before commitment can doom a relationship. Such is the absolute balance of this procreative universe. The sexual embrace is a holy act; the most holy, and it cannot be treated in any other way, at least not without serious consequences. This whole approach to sex education being promoted today, the use of condoms, oral sex, homosexual acts, etc., completely misses the point of the sacredness of the sexual act. If we want to grow up and grow beyond Christianity, Humanism, and Homosexuality, we would view the sexual embrace in its holy (procreative) nature. In fact, that is all we need to do. But to do so, wouldn't we have to be accountable for *life?* Ah, there is the problem, isn't it? *Do you want to be accountable for life?* Christianity, Humanism, and Homosexuality say no. Man and Woman Balance says *yes.*

This writing was written some twenty or so years ago. In this short time the homosexual movement has morphed into LGBTP*Q. What this (Q) really means is that there isn't a 1st Principle/Absolute and so anything goes thus everything must be legal, praised, and even funded, whether it be LGBTPQ education of children in the public schools to the killing of babies to the advocation and legislation of pedophilia. Probably one of the most revealing terms within the LGBTPQ movement is the term Genderqueer. This means, and I am quoting from a definition of Genderqueer I ran across online, *"a gender identity that is fluid, changing, or exists between binary categories of man and woman."* Well, can we just make things up, create "new categories" whenever one feels dissatisfied with the current smorgasbord of choices? Can 2 + 2 = 5 or maybe 7 whenever one prefers it to? Or is this universe one of absolutes, where 2 + 2 always equals 4, where sex is binary (equal and opposite) and male and female are the only categories available in LIFE?

*P stands for pedophilia.

In Christianity, and other religious persuasions, it is suggested we are born into original sin. Due to the fall of Adam and Eve, each one of us has a sin upon our souls that, it is believed, we cannot undo by ourselves alone. Thus, the need for a "saviour." In contrast to this line of thinking lies Transcendentalism (perhaps the Western term for Eastern thought) that runs through some religions and various philosophies. (The New Age movement of the last number of years is essentially Transcendentalism.) Transcendentalism says that our souls are already perfect and complete if we would just recognize this. But, unfortunately, it does not make the sexual distinction (equal and opposite) between man and woman and, as such, loses its point of balance. What we call original sin is just a point of imbalance. As earlier stated: *One is not without the other; both are needed for either to be.*

Homosexuality*

Original Sin Verses Spiritual Perfection

To date, each of us has been born into a one-force consciousness. Our controlling metaphysic has been imbalanced. One could call this imbalance *sin*. But the answer to this is not necessarily to tap into the "spiritual perfection" of Transcendentalism, or some "Savior." I agree that our logos/ soul is perfect, but its perfection lies in its balance. We are not individually perfected per se. We are perfected/completed in our balance with our equal and opposite other half, i.e., *procreatively* perfected. Too often today, I see people who proclaim that they are complete or whole unto themselves alone. We are not. One just need ask oneself whether or not one can make a baby by oneself alone, cloning notwithstanding. We are not singular beings. We are sexual beings in an eternal relationship with our equal and opposite other half. Our completeness or wholeness lies in our *procreative balance together*. The mistake of Christianity lies in the misunderstanding of our eternal balance together. But the solution lies not in the idea/belief that some saviour is coming to our rescue. We rise or fall solely upon the recognition of our balance together with our equal and opposite other half. In other words, our spiritual perfection/salvation lies in our procreative balance together, equal and opposite, male and female, man and woman. In this statement we see that the idea of spiritual procreation transcends both Christianity and Transcendentalism (or Eastern thought).

So, it is man and woman balance that destroys the mis-premise of original sin and its one-force hierarchical structure that supports it. It actually destroys all forms of victimization. We, in our balance, are centered on our *primary action*. Call this the Golden Rule, cause/effect, the law of karma, balance, or attraction, each of us, in our balance together, are the source of our thought/action from which the reaction comes perfectly back to us. You might say, we only act unto our other half from which that exact and perfect reaction comes back to us from our other half. Yet, how many of us today act out of reaction, from what we proclaim is happening to us? "So and so is doing it to me," or "It's the system's fault," or "It's the racism or sexism or fascism structured into the society," or "My parents did it to me," or "Nobody understands or accepts me," etc. We can come up with hundreds of reasons/excuses. Yet, the victim mentality always results in powerlessness. And what does powerlessness result in? How about rage or bitterness or depression or envy or revenge, to name a few things? But we can never break out of the victim mentality as long as we fail to understand the balance that exists between each one of us via the man and woman relationship. All the New Age work on transforming oneself to the "higher self" has failed to materialize because this basic (procreative) balance was not understood. Again, we have fallen into the trap of victimization. We cannot purify our initial action such that we can embrace all of the reactions that come back to us. In a way, we are still trapped in "original sin." As such, we have yet to touch the eternal—*in each other*—and are left wanting. There is only one solution to this "problem of the ages" that has haunted all of mankind since the beginning. We must understand the source of our eternal life.

Spiritual Procreation and Eternal Life

Hopefully, by now, you will have gathered that spiritual procreation is another word for *eternal life*. To date, we have never recognized that eternal life is not singular, even on the spiritual level. There must be the *procreant* or *perpetual creative* aspect to it. Spiritual procreation is that *procreant* or *perpetual creative* aspect. It recognizes the two forces as eternal *together*, eternal in their *procreation. It's the lineage, you know!* Yes, we do come through our parents and live through our children! In other words, *we aren't saved by ourselves alone (or some "higher power"); we are only saved as procreative pairs, i.e., man and woman—and a child is born!*

This idea of a dual salvation is very difficult for many people to accept. It means that each one of us has to hold to the balance that exists between each of us and our other half at this very moment. Indeed, that is the reality. Surrender to it; it is not going away. But what about the Christian (or Muslim, Jew, Hindu, or Buddhist, etc.); or the Humanist, Socialist, Communist, Democrat, or Republican; or the Homosexual, Bi-sexual, or Transgender person; or the "whole transcendent, androgynous, perfected, singular "spirit"; or the newborn child brought up in hopelessness and despair, or the widowed old man or woman waiting to die? What about everybody? Pray *The Eternal Prayer*. (*The Eternal Prayer* is listed in the chapter *The Four Explanative Drawings of Spiritual Procreation*.) Pray it today. Pray it now. What else is there? Do you want an eternal life answer? Pray *The Eternal Prayer*. It will cleanse your soul—*forever*. And in that moment, you will hear your other half speak to you. *I am here. I have always been here just for you*. And you will know that this is true and, in response, can finally say, *I believe in us*.

Equation for Eternal Life

Given that Man and Woman Balance = Procreative Love,
and Procreative Love = the Survival of the Species
or Perpetual Creation, and Perpetual Creation =
Eternal Life; thus Man and Woman Balance = Eternal Life

Eternal Life

Philosophical Investigations

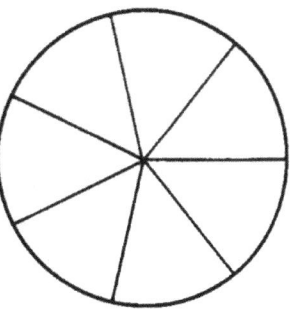

Let us begin this section with a quote on the purpose of philosophy.

Ray Kotobuki— *The Philosophical Zero*
"The physicist-mathematician Sir James Jeans (1877-1946) cogently defined science as 'the earnest attempt to set in order the facts of experience.' Philosophy is a sphere of science that deals with 'order' itself; it is the science or knowledge of the principles of 'ordering' the facts of experience. Philosophy permeates the entire field of science and provides the principle or the context in which to set in order the given facts of experience that pertain to a particular branch of science. Without a valid philosophical foundation, no branch of science could arrive at a valid picture or theory of the reality-sphere about which it is concerned….

"Philosophy, thus, concerns itself with the principle of 'ordering' and provides a contextual order for all branches of science and all spheres of human existence…. Philosophy, therefore, is the reflection or expression of the fundamental inner working of consciousness qua consciousness. No philosophy has ever existed before the advent of consciousness. The bicameral mind had various myths but not a single philosophy….

"To be human, to be conscious, in essence is to be a philosopher and what kind of philosophy one consciously or subconsciously possesses determines the entire destiny of his life. Similarly, what kind of philosophy humanity as a whole predominantly chooses determines the entire course of human history."

"…what kind of philosophy humanity as a whole predominantly chooses determines the entire course of human history." Powerful words. It appears that our own (personal) philosophy, which can be generally thought of as our fundamental belief system, determines the entire course of our own lives. As I view it, philosophy is the pursuit of an absolute. Its intention, or should I say my intention or your intention, is to ascertain the fundamental order of things. We might call this the pursuit of a Universal Order—if there is one. But must there not be an objective order that we <u>can</u> comprehend and <u>must</u> comprehend for our very lives? If there isn't a Universal

Order, well then, we could not think. Mind/thought would not be. The sad part is that philosophy, I believe, has given up on its pursuit of an absolute, what I also call a **Metaphysical Absolute** or a **Metaphysical Given**. Listen to the words of Paul Strathern from his writing *Socrates in 90 Minutes*. I have drawn from his book in creating this lineage.

Paul Strathern—*Socrates in 90 Minutes*

"It has taken philosophers twenty-five centuries of getting it wrong to conclude that getting it wrong isn't the point. Now they believe that the mere practice of philosophy is what matters. Thus, philosophy has become an activity, like wine-tasting or tax evasion, with similarly ambiguous effects on the practitioner. For the first time in the history of philosophy, the attempt by any individual to construct a philosophy as such has become redundant. The tradition of Plato, Kant, Ehrensvard, and Wittgenstein has come to an end. This tradition of reason and observation, which attracted some of the finest minds the world has known, first grew to maturity with Socrates."

This investigation will be a lineage of philosophy taking quotes from various philosophers down through the ages. I certainly will not be able to cover all the primary philosophers, but I hope you can capture a flavor of what has happened to philosophy and, as a result, the difficulties we now face. Some of the philosophers I will cite by using just a short quote; others longer or many quotes. It all depends on the idea(s) I want to convey, and the length or number of quotes I use is not to be construed as a reflection on the greatness, or lack thereof, of that particular philosopher. After the philosopher's quote(s), I follow with my own analysis focusing on the issue of the **Metaphysical Absolute /Metaphysical Given.** But even more specific than that, what is the missing yet most fundamental idea/reality—without which there cannot even be LIFE? Hold to that question as we progress through this Investigation.

Lastly, I would like to state that I myself am not a philosopher. I did major in Philosophy and Humanistic Psychology in college. But, as has been said, getting a degree in anything is just a beginning. In recent years my interest has moved towards the New Thought Movement. I have been most affected by the writings of Walter Russell, a scientist, philosopher, and artist. Not surprising then, I do include in this Investigation quotes from Dr. Russell and his wife Lao Russell.

Socrates (469 B.C.-399 B.C.)
"Dear Agathon, it is truth you cannot contradict. You can easily contradict Socrates." Plato, *Symposium*
"Everything has one opposite and not more than one." Plato, *Protagoras*.

Socrates is a safe place to begin as he is considered the father of Western philosophy. I have chosen a most simple yet profound quote from him as recorded by Plato. *"It is truth you cannot contradict,"* is the basis of Western philosophy and civilization. Implied in this quote is that there is a universal/eternal truth, i.e., a metaphysical reality or "what is" and that it cannot be contradicted. What is, *is*. The conception of a truth is the foundation of our consciousness. It arises out of the abstraction of a one order. Truth fits into the idea that consciousness is conceptual. It is our (one and only) task to derive this truth. The second quote by Socrates is, perhaps, the most succinct quote in all philosophy, the basis of the two-force paradigm. If only we could have known.

Plato (427 B.C.-348 B.C.)
"Suppose that when someone sees or hears or notices something he says to himself: 'What I perceive looks rather like something else, though it is in fact only a poor imitation.' Don't you agree that the person who receives this impression must have had previous knowledge of that 'something else,' and is in fact being reminded of it? ...Then we must have had some earlier knowledge of equality before we first saw things which were almost equal, without being fully so...and at the same time we agree that we did not and could not have come by this notion of equality except by sight or touch or one of the senses. I am treating them as all being the same.... So it must be by the senses that we become aware of the notion that things which are almost

equal are not absolutely equal. Yet we must have a notion of this absolute equality, or there would be no standard with which to compare the things that we perceive as being almost equal...but surely we first see and hear and use our senses only at birth? ...But previously we agreed that we must have knowledge of equivalence and nonequivalence before we use our senses, or we would not be able to make any sense of them.... Which means we must have had this knowledge before we were born.... Therefore, if we had this knowledge before we were born, and knew it when we were born, this means we had knowledge not only of equality and relative equivalence, but also of all absolute standards. And this same argument which we applied to absolute equality, applies just as much to the absolutes of beauty, goodness, morality, and holiness. And also, I maintain, to all those characteristics to which we apply the term 'absolute.' This shows that we must obtain knowledge of such absolutes before we were born." *Phaedo*

Plato is suggesting that the absolute (truth) is something we know innately. He uses the term "before we were born." We could say we know the truth universally; it is eternal to us or within us — *the logos*. Plato is known for his idea of universal forms (ideas). He suggested that the universal was the real. Plato has been criticized for suggesting a split between the universal and the temporal world we find ourselves within. The criticism is that we can't really know this so-called universal world of forms and, therefore, it is "metaphysical" or "transcendental" invoking a "detached (one-force) presence." Accordingly, to seek this "presence" then actually takes us out of this world. Yet, as I understand Plato, he did suggest that we can, and should, connect to the forms (truth) through reason. It is in our reason that we can know the truth, especially given the fact that the universal (as his quote indicates) is also already within us.

Aristotle (384 B.C.-322 B.C.)
"All men by nature desire to know." *Metaphysics*

"But he who knows best about each genus must be able to state the most certain principles of his subject, so that he whose subject is being *qua* being must be able to state the most certain principles of all things. This is the philosopher, and the most certain principle of all is that regarding which it is impossible to be mistaken; for such a principle must be both the best known (for all men may be mistaken about things which they do not know), and non-hypothetical. For a principle which everyone must have who knows anything about being, is not a hypothesis; and that which everyone must know who knows anything, he must already have when he comes to a special study. Evidently then such a principle is the most certain of all; which principle this is, we proceed to say. It is, that the same attribute cannot at the same time belong and not belong to the same subject in the same respect; we must presuppose, in face of dialectical objections, any further qualifications which might be added. This, then, is the most certain of all principles, since it answers to the definition given above. For it is impossible for anyone to believe the same thing to be and not to be, as some think Heraclitus says; for what a man says he does not necessarily believe. If it is impossible that contrary attributes should belong at the same time to the same subject (the usual qualifications must be presupposed in the proposition too), and if an opinion which contradicts another is contrary to it, obviously it is impossible for the same man at the same time to believe the same thing to be and not to be; for if a man were mistaken in this point, he would have contrary opinions at the same time. It is for this reason that all who are carrying out a demonstration refer it to this as an ultimate belief; for this is naturally the starting-point even for all the other axioms." *Metaphysics*

I have chosen two quotes from Aristotle. First, we see Aristotle confirming Socrates in a way asserting a knowledge or truth. In the second quote, we see Aristotle present the (logical) argument that our knowledge must be based in non-contradictory logic, i.e., a self-evident truth/axiom. Aristotle uses the principles of identity, non-contradiction, and the excluded middle which are all variations of what I call identity-in-relationship. Aristotle actually gives to us the principles (or laws) that we must follow to properly abstract although, as I have indicated, they are not quite complete. In doing so, he gives to us our epistemological vehicle through which we may touch the metaphysical/eternal. Indeed, the truth is there but it just does not come to us through some primary faith or experience; we must abstract for it. This is what it means to say that consciousness is conceptual.

St. Augustine (354-430)

"There was no extreme of heat or cold in paradise, and its inhabitants experienced no desire or fear which might obstruct their goodwill.... A man and his wife maintained a faithful partnership based on love and mutual respect, and faultless observance of the commandment.... When humanity was blessed with such ease and plenty, it would have been possible for the seed of children to be sown unaccompanied by foul lust. The sexual organs would have been stimulated into necessary activity by willpower alone, just as the will controls other organs. Then, without being goaded on by the allurement of passion, the husband could have relaxed upon his wife's bosom in complete peace of mind and bodily tranquility...that part of his body not activated by tumultuous passion, but brought into service by the deliberate use of power when the need arose, the seed dispatched into the womb with no loss of his wife's virginity....So the two sexes could have come together for impregnation and conception by an act of will, rather than by lustful cravings." *City of God*

I have chosen this quote from Augustine because it brings in the man and woman relationship and its act of procreation, showing it to be something other or higher than our lusts. Augustine was concerned with rising above his own lusts as well as solving the problem of evil. He actually is known for his synthesis of Christian and Platonic thought. Like Plotinus before him, he believed that our innermost spirits were linked to, or even one with, the light of God (what I would call procreative balance) and that our task was to surrender or unify with this light (I would say to unify with our other half). Our innermost spirits (under rational constrain), are also where we find the universal forms of Plato, one of them being the good. Now, when we bring this light of God or the good to our relationships, we can connect (eternally)—our touch will be spiritual (procreative love) rather than simply physical which Augustine calls lust. Today we would call lust by the name pornography which, by definition, is physical sex without spiritual union. Augustine is making a distinction between the two suggesting that "sex of the will" does not tarnish our souls as does lust.

Thomas Aquinas (1225-1274)

"The purpose of each thing is that which is intended by the creator or mover of that thing. Now the prime mover or creator of the universe is spirit or mind. For this reason the final end or purpose of the universe must be the good of the intellect. And this is truth. Thus truth must be the final purpose of the universe, and the pondering of truth must be the chief occupation of wisdom." *Summa contra Gentiles: The Activity of the Wise*

A short quote from such a prolific writer but it contains so much. Whereas St. Augustine attempted to synthesize Plato and Christianity, Thomas Aquinas attempted to synthesize Aristotle and Christianity. He sought to bring the viability of reason to Christian faith. This is the purpose of his argument for a first creator or prime mover, that there must be, at some point, a 1st cause and we can know this through our reason. He also brought back around Aristotle's teleological view that there is a fundamental purpose to things, in Aquinas' view, that of the truth. Truth is our purpose; what a profound idea. Now, I must take a moment here and outline the problem with Thomas Aquinas and those who came before him. We find in this quote such (singular) ideas as prime mover, spirit, and mind. Here we have the "detached presence" again, that non- relational (one-force) term(s) that hasn't definition or meaning. Things only have meaning in relation to other things. Now, what is interesting is that Aristotle actually brought forth a two-force, non-contradictory, epistemology (that we are now completing). It is this epistemology that Aquinas sought to synthesize with Christianity. But neither Aristotle's or Aquinas' epistemology, for the reasons we are discussing, sunk its way back into metaphysics, even given Socrates claim that everything had its opposite. Later philosophers attack and actually collapse philosophy (specifically metaphysics) on this point of a "detached presence," some singular "oneness" that is purported to exist behind everything but that we can never really know. Indeed. Our "rationalism" is still one-force to this day and our empiricism, rather than correcting this problem with the understanding of a one order plus a two forces, collapses the idea of an absolute altogether and leaves us in relativism.

Niccolo Machiavelli (1469-1527)

"It is necessary for anyone establishing a state and setting down its laws to presuppose that all people are evil, and that they will always act according to the wickedness of their spirits whenever they get the chance." *Discourses*

Machiavelli is actually a political philosopher. He shows to us the naked truth of politics and human nature. His writing *The Prince* is a depiction of what a prince (or politician) must assume and act upon to secure power. Now, this doesn't have much to do with our conversation at this point concerning metaphysics or epistemology. Politics falls into the ethical arena of philosophy. But I want to bring up this point to you, which is, that without a metaphysics, specifically the two-force metaphysics of man and woman balance, we cannot have an ethics, i.e., what are called unalienable rights, those universal/eternal checks and balances on the small (evil) side of both politics and human nature. The unalienable rights that we supposedly have today are based on a one-force "God," a "God" which, by its nature, is imbalanced. The so-called political/human rights we have are based on the relativity of empiricism (and the superiority of the state) which denies the delineation between rights and needs. In either case we are not free and will never be until we balance our metaphysics.

Rene Descartes (1596-1650)

"It is some time since I first realized how many false opinions I accepted as true from my childhood, and how doubtful was the entire structure of thought which I had built upon them. I therefore understood that I must, if I wanted to establish anything at all in science that was firm and liable to last, once and for all rid myself of all the opinions I had adopted, and start from an entirely new foundation." *Meditations*

"The long chains of simple and easy reasonings, which geometers use to reach the most difficult conclusions, had given me reason to suppose that all things which can be known by humanity are connected in some way. And that there is nothing so far removed from us as to be beyond our reach, or so hidden that we cannot discover it, as long as we abstain from accepting the false for the true, and always preserve in our thoughts the order necessary for the deduction of one truth from another. Also, I had little difficulty in determining the objects with which it was necessary to commence, for I was already convinced that these must be the simplest and easiest known." *Discourse on Method, Part II*

"Since I desired to devote myself wholly to the search for truth, I thought it necessary...to reject as if utterly false anything in which I could discover the least grounds for doubt, so that I could find out if I was left with anything at all which was absolutely indubitable. Thus, because our senses sometimes deceive us, I decided to suppose that nothing was really as they led us to believe it was. And, because some of us make mistakes in reasoning, committing logical errors in even the simplest matters of geometry, I rejected as erroneous all reasonings that I had previously taken as proofs. And finally, when I considered that the very same things we perceive when we are awake may also occur to us while we are asleep and not perceiving anything at all, I resolved to pretend that anything that had ever entered my mind was no more than a dream. But immediately I noticed that while I was thinking in this way, and regarding everything as false, it was nonetheless absolutely necessary that I, who was doing this thinking, was still something. And observing that this truth, 'I think, therefore I am,' (*Cogito, ergo sum*) was so sure and certain that no ground for doubt, be it ever so extravagantly skeptical, was capable of shaking it, I therefore decided that I could accept it without scruple as the 1st principle of the philosophy I was seeking to create." *Discourse on Method, Part IV*

Well, I had to pick three quotes from Descartes. He is considered to be the father of modern philosophy. You can see the shift in him compared to previous religious philosophers. He is looking for a point in certainty within himself through the vehicle of his reason. Descartes, we would say, was a rationalist, but his rationalism was not to be based on some "detached presence" but on his own analysis. In reading these quotes where he finally gets down to a 1st principle, an axiom of his own certainty, we see a lot of Aristotle. Descartes was looking for a deductive process of sound reasoning such that anything could be investigated. Now, the question remains, did he find that process or center of things? Is our reasoning and certainty based on "I think, therefore I am"? Well, perhaps in a one-force universe where A is A. But where is B? How about altering the *Cogito* a bit to say, "I, in relation to you, think (also in relation to you), therefore *we* are.

Baruch Spinoza (1632-1677)

> I. By CAUSE OF ITSELF (*causa sui*) I understand that whose essence involves existence; or that whose nature cannot be conceived except as existing.
>
> II. A thing is said to be FINITE IN ITS KIND (*in suo genere finita*) when it can be limited by another thing of the same nature. For example, a body is said to be finite because we can always conceive of another body larger than it. Similarly, thought is limited by another thought. But body cannot be limited by thought, nor thought by body.
>
> III. By SUBSTANCE (*substantia*) I understand that which is in itself and is conceived through itself. That is, that the conception of which does not depend upon the conception of another thing, from which it has to be formed.
>
> IV. By ATTRIBUTE (*attributum*) I understand that which the intellect perceives of substance as constituting its essence.
>
> V. By MODE (*modus*) I understand the modification of substance; that which is in something else,

through which it is also conceived.

VI. By GOD (*Deus*) I understand an absolutely infinite being, that is, substance consisting of infinite attributes, each of which expresses eternal and infinite essence.

VII. A thing is said to be FREE (*libera*) which exists solely through the necessity of its own nature, and is determined into action by itself alone. That thing is said to be NECESSARY (*necessaria*) or rather COMPELLED (*coacta*), which is determined by something else to exist and act in a certain definite and determinate way.

VIII. I understand ETERNITY (*aetenitas*) in so far as it is conceived as following necessarily from the definition of an eternal thing. *Ethics, Part 1*

"Truth is the standard of itself and the false." B. Spinoza

"When people think they are free, they are deceived. They hold to this opinion only because they are conscious of their actions but remain ignorant of what actually causes these actions." *Ethics, Part 2*

Spinoza is also a rationalist. You can see from the first quote his logical analysis. He, too, is attempting to get down to a 1st principle or cause which he calls *substance*. We see in Spinoza some of the method of Aristotle to reach some of the metaphysical conclusions of Plato (or Plotinus). Spinoza seeks the one order/truth universally or eternally. Descartes would be too individualistic for him, I think. And yet, what if we combined the two? You see, this whole debate or dilemma is due to the metaphysical difference between order and force. Yes, there can be a one order (which Descartes fails to adequately address) but there must be two forces (which Spinoza fails to address). I like Spinoza because of the sense of the eternal he brings to his philosophy. He also has some devastating quotes on truth and freedom. In the first, he is saying that the truth is its own standard; it is the given that illuminates and measures all things. In the last quote Spinoza suggests we don't understand what the underlying motivations are to our actions. So how can we possibly be (spiritually) free? Do we even have a clue that we are absolutely controlled by our metaphysics which, to date, has been premised on the mis-premise of a one force or, more recently, the denial of an absolute altogether i.e. relativism?

John Locke (1632-1704)

"There are (no innate principles) to which all mankind give a universal consent. I shall begin with the speculative, an instance in those magnified principles of demonstration, *Whatsoever is, is* and *It is impossible for the same thing to be and not to be,* which of all others I think have the most allowed title to innate. These have so settled a reputation of maxims universally received that it will, no doubt, be thought strange if anyone should seem to question it. But yet I take the liberty to say that these propositions are so far from having a universal assent, that there are a great part of mankind to who they are not so much as known.... For, first, it is evident that all *children* and *idiots* have not the least apprehension or thought of them." *An Essay Concerning Human Understanding*

"The *natural liberty* of man is to be free from any superior power on earth, and not to be under the will or legislative authority of man, but to have only the law of nature for his rule. The liberty of man, in society, is to be under no other legislative power but that established, by consent, in the commonwealth, nor under the dominion of any will, or restraint of any law, but what the legislative will enact, according to the trust put in it." *Two Treatises of Government*

In John Locke we see the beginning of the end for rationalism. In the first quote above, he lays the groundwork for empiricism. He is suggesting that there aren't any innate (universal) principles or self-evident logic systems, that what knowledge we may have is therefore based on our experience. Locke believed in the scientific method and the inductive process that was gaining favor during his time. We attain our understanding of the world, not through some detached rationalism/speculation but through the concrete of our experience. For example, we come to the idea of an apple not through some innate knowledge of the *idea* apple but by perceiving/experiencing apples and then deducing the idea *apple*. This idea is hard to argue with and yet it has immense consequences. If nothing else, it does away with the idea of an absolute truth. Locke is known for the idea of *tabula rasa* (blank slate) which means we begin life from nothing. There isn't an eternal light or logos in our spirits coming in. We only know or gain from what we experience. But, let us ask, what is experience? It is loosely defined as information gained from the senses rather than from reason. This means it is information gained from looking outward rather than inward. But let me ask, is experience somehow neutral? Does it come to us pure in form giving to us all its information without distortion? Perhaps we are also involved in this process by how we *interpret* our experience dependent on the metaphysical (internal structure) we hold. The empiricists hold (the idea) experience in some a priori/mystical/non-challengeable status (the same criticism they have of the rationalists concerning innate ideas), when they can't even present or explain the basis for correct interpretation of experience—through *1st principles, logic, and axioms*. As such, taken to its logical conclusion, experience, as a methodology, leaves us in relativity. What Locke failed to see was that (innate) ideas and experiential (things) come together. It is the chicken/egg dichotomy we discussed earlier. Ideas and things are opposites in relationship. *One is not without the other; both are needed for either to be.* As such they come together or not at all. There aren't any domains of "pure idea" or "pure thing." As I have said, I am not suggesting we dismiss empiricism in favor of a singular separate rationalism. I am suggesting we consider both. A singular separate rationalism often results in some kind of dogmatic blind faith. A singular separate empiricism results in relativity. Both are the result of the one-force mis-premise.

Having gotten through my dislike of Locke's empiricism, let's take a moment and look at his second quote on natural liberty. That is a great quote. If Thomas Jefferson is the father of our country, certainly John Locke is the grandfather. We are to be under the thumb of no one; no masters and no slaves is what arises from the metaphysical balance of man and woman. Now, I wonder if the idea of the *law of nature* is innate or from experience for Locke. Is it absolute or relative? Hmm.

Gottfried Wilhelm Leibniz (1646-1716)

"The monad, of which we shall speak here, is nothing but a simple substance which enters into compounds, simple, that is to say, without parts.... There must be simple substances, because there are compounds; for the compound is nothing but a collection or aggregate of simples.... Where there are no parts, neither extension, shape, nor divisibility is possible. And these monads are the true atoms of nature. In a word, they are the elements of things....

"There is no way of explaining how a monad can be altered or changed with itself by any other created thing, since it is impossible to move anything in it or to conceive of the possibility of any internal motion being started. Such a motion could neither be started, given direction, increased, nor decreased within it, as can take place in compounds, where change among the parts can take place. Monads have no windows by which anything could come in or go out." *Monadology*

"Each monad (or substance) has something of the infinite, in that it involves its cause: God. That is to say, it has some trace of omniscience and omnipotence. For in the perfect notion of each individual substance there are contained all its predicates, both necessary and contingent, as well as its past, present, and future. Each monad (or substance) expresses the whole universe according to its situation and aspect, in so far as things are referred to it. Thus it is necessary that some of our perceptions, be they ever so clear, remain confused, since they involve things which are infinite....

"The notion of a pre-established harmony results from the notion of monads (or substance). For according to this, the idea of each monad (or substance) involves all that will ever happen to it....True, there is a miracle involved in the system of pre-established harmony. But this is only the beginning, where God enters into it. After this everything goes its own way in the phenomena of nature, according to the laws of souls and bodies....This hypothesis is not gratuitous, even though it cannot be proved a priori." *Collected Writings*

"Regarding the proposition that three is equal to two plus one—this is only the definition of the term three. It is true that this contains a hidden proposition: namely, that the ideas of these numbers are possible. Here this is known intuitively, this we can say that intuitive knowledge is contained in definitions when their possibility is immediately evident." *Monadology*

"Primitive truths, which are known by means of intuition, are of two kinds. They are either truths of reason, or truths of fact. Truths of reason are necessary, this is to say, they cannot be denied: their opposite is impossible. Truths of fact are contingent. That is to say, their opposite is possible. Primitive truths of reason are those which I call by the general name of 'identicals,' because it seems they only repeat the same thing in a different manner, without teaching us anything. Those which are affirmative are such as the following: 'Everything is what is,' 'A is A, B is B,' 'The equilateral rectangle is a rectangle.'...Now we come to the negative identicals, which depend either upon the principle of contradiction or upon that of disparates. The principle of contradiction is in general: A proposition is either true or false." *Collected Writings*

"Our reasoning is founded on two great principles: the principle of contradiction, or, what comes to the same thing, that of identity.... Secondly there is the principle of sufficient reason, by virtue of which we consider that no fact can be real or existing, and no proposition can be true unless there is a sufficient reason why it should be thus and not otherwise, even though in most cases these reasons cannot be known to us." *Monadology*

What do you make out of these quotes by Leibniz? He actually was a child genius who later invented integral and differential calculus. As I understand it, his concept of the monad was as a point of energy. What I like about his idea of the monad (what I might call the soul) is that each monad expresses the idea of the whole universe in a pre-established harmony. We see both Plato and Spinoza in play here. Let's say that within each of us is the perfect logos or design of the universe which we, man and woman, *procreatively*, play out in perfect balance together. Each monad (male or female) is from the "beginning," dividing and uniting in eternal procreative process. Well, I don't think Leibniz went this far. His monads were essentially singular (not sexed) rather than procreative. His epistemology is also interesting. We see Aristotle here, the principles of identity and non-contradiction. We also see that Leibniz understood *intuitively* that the beginning point of conceptual understanding comes from a non-provable given. He also presents us with the idea of sufficient reason which is a similar idea to initial purpose. Leibniz is a rationalist of the first order, unfortunately mostly forgotten today because his ideas (of monads) do not fit in with the "experience is everything" philosophy of today.

George Berkeley (1685-1753)

"It is evident to anyone who takes a survey of the objects of human knowledge, that they are either ideas imprinted on the senses, or else such as are perceived by attending to the passions and operations of the mind, or lastly ideas formed by help of memory and imagination, either compounding, dividing, or barely representing those originally perceived in the aforesaid ways…. But besides all that endless variety of ideas or objects of knowledge, there is likewise something which knows or perceives them, and exercises divers operations, as willing, imagining, remembering about them. This perceiving, active being is what I call *mind, spirit, soul or myself.* By which words I do not denote any one of my ideas, but a thing entirely distinct from them, wherein they exist, or, which is the same thing, whereby they are perceived; for the existence of an idea consists in being perceived." *A Treatise Concerning the Principles of Human Knowledge, Part 1*

With Berkeley we continue the empiricist track that Locke had revived. Berkeley takes Locke a step further indicating that since, supposedly, all we have is our experience, i.e., our perception; that the essence of our being is to be perceived. Berkeley is known by his famous statement—*to be is to be perceived*. Notice how perception here is even primary to ourselves. Berkeley posits an active being that perceives (mind, spirit, soul, or self—or even "God") in an attempt to create some primary. But then we again have the one-force misconception in play. Now, I wonder if the focus here should be on our perceiving rather than our being perceived. If Berkeley had said to be is to perceive, we would see more of a linkage to conceptual consciousness. Now, I am not denying the necessity of perception but that is only one-half of the story. We also conceive. *To be is to conceive.* (This is the big denial that is occurring in the world today.) For one to be conscious it is not enough to just perceive/experience. One must also conceive/abstract. Animals perceive. We, humans, conceive. We must make that first abstraction of a one order. We must also make the second abstraction of a two forces.

David Hume (1711-1776)

"Thus not only our reason fails us in the discovery of the *ultimate connexion* of causes and effects, but even after experience has inform'd us of their *constant conjunction,* 'tis impossible for us to satisfy ourselves by our reason, why shou'd extend that experience beyond those particular instances, which have fallen under our observation. We suppose, but we are never able to prove, that there must be a resemblance betwixt those objects, of which we have had experience, and those which lie beyond the reach of our discovery." *A Treatise of Human Nature,* Book 1

Hume takes Berkeley to the empiricist "logical" conclusion. Since we (supposedly) only experience/perceive, how can we logically deduce anything—such as "God" for example? Hume's historical example was that of cause and effect. According to Hume, we cannot deduce a causal connection between things because we do not perceive that. Indeed, we don't. We actually only perceive the sense data in the immediate moment. We must make that causal connection ourselves. But can we do this with certainty? Yes, with all the certainty that is contained in the statement that *consciousness is conceptual* or that there are *two forces to creation*. Now, if we are to hold experience as a priori Hume wins. Logic (causality/the law of balance) breaks down. But if we hold the deeper view that we can conceive (that there is an order—of two forces—to conception which is the same order of the universe itself) then, indeed, we can know with absolute certainty that there is a (procreative) connection between things—like between a man and a woman and their child.

Jean-Jacques Rousseau (1712-1777)

"The first man who enclosed a piece of land, who then came up with the idea of saying 'this is mine' and found people simple enough to believe him, was the true founder of civil society. How many crimes, wars and murders stem from this act? How much misery and horror the human race would have been spared if someone had simply pulled out the stakes and filled in the ditch and cried out to his fellow men: 'Beware of listening to this imposter. You are lost if you forget that the fruits of the earth belong to everyone and that the earth itself belongs to no one!'"
Discourse on the Origin of Inequality

It probably should not surprise you if I tell you that I am not a big fan of Rousseau. He set in motion the principle and spirit of the French and Russian Revolutions, which were revolutions against private property. For a free system to exist we must have unalienable rights which, in effect, means the right to earn and own what one earns. It does not mean some "right to possess" just because one exits or is part of some group or cause. There is another issue of concern here. Unalienable rights/private property actually arise out of the deeper position that consciousness is conceptual. It is a conceptual consciousness that can make those necessary abstractions. If we are to hold to the position that consciousness is perceptual/experiential, we cannot make the abstractions so necessary for freedom. (The abstraction between rights and needs and the necessity of individual productive effort, for example.) We are left with the fog of pure experience and group solidarity, or in Rousseau words from other writings, the "general will." "We are all one" and "power to the people," the group mass shouts while denying the basis of the conceptual process, which itself requires *effort*.

Immanuel Kant (1724-1804)

"Time has no objective reality; it is not an accident, not a substance, and not a relation: it is a purely subjective condition, necessary because of the nature of the human mind, which coordinates all our sensibilities by a certain law, and is a pure intuition. We coordinate substance and accidents alike, according to simultaneity and succession, only through the concept of time." *Collected Works, Vol. 2*

With Kant we see the effort to restore metaphysics from the Locke/Berkeley/Hume assault. What Kant essentially said was that experience is not metaphysically free. He agreed with the essentiality of experience but argued in his *Critique of Pure Reason* that experience conforms to our knowledge (conception), not the other way around. You can see in the above quote the idea of the nature of the human mind. Kant said that we perceive/interpret the world through the categories of our minds. For example, causality. That is how we see things because that is how our minds work—*by a certain law*. I don't have any problem with this idea except that Kant further suggested that through the "rose-colored" glasses of our conception (categories) we don't actually see the real world. He said that we only see the phenomenon of the world, not the noumenon ("God") or "true reality." (Isn't the "certain law" true reality?) Well, where does this leave us? We might as well return to the sole experience of relativity. Perhaps our conceptual categories are the way the world works. That is certainly the case in the two-force paradigm. The metaphysical and epistemological processes are one and the same. There really isn't a (singular) noumenon (unless we are referring to order) if you will. That idea is part and parcel of a one-force world where we keep looking for some ultimate (singular) building block to all things. The world of phenomenon (relationship) is the real world—coordinated by a certain universal law known as sexual balance.

Georg Wilhelm Friedrich Hegel (1770-1832)

"Every true or real logical thought has three aspects. Firstly, the abstract or comprehensible aspect, which indicates what a thing is. Secondly, its dialectical negation, which says what it is not.

Thirdly, the speculative—which is concrete comprehension: *A* is at the same time that which it is not. These three aspects do not constitute the three aspects of logic; rather they are moments of everything which has logical reality and truth. They are part of every philosophical concept. Every concept is rational, is an abstraction opposed to another, and is comprehended by a unity with its opposite. This is the definition of the dialectic." *The Encyclopedia of the Philosophical Sciences in Outline*

Hegel brings us back to the dialectical method of Plato and Aristotle. You might say that Hegel is saying that the categories of the mind constitute the dialectic process itself. Hegel's famous dialectic is that of thesis—anti-thesis—synthesis. This itself is the sexual (procreative) process, although he didn't make that further abstraction. It is interesting here that Hegel suggests that everything (per the dialectic) has logical reality and truth. The implication here is that metaphysical reality is this dialectical process. "God," or Kant's noumenon, is a process (verb) not a singular thing (noun). Hegel actually makes the more correct restoration of metaphysics than Kant in giving to us the two-force process as ultimate (logical and knowable) reality. And yet, Hegel makes the same mistake Kant made. Hegel gives to us the singular (unknowable) Absolute Spirit that supposedly is the grand synthesis of all things. Here we see the attempt to hang on to the "detached presence" that has been the death blow to rationality and metaphysics. Can't we have a rationality and metaphysics free from this one-force mis-premise; one that fully embraces Life itself?

Arthur Schopenhauer (1788-1860)
"Only at one point do I have access to the world other than as representation. This is in myself. When I perceive my body, this is representation...but I am also aware of those urges which give rise to this representation: this is Will. Only within myself do I have this dual knowledge of Will and representation." *The World as Will and Representation*

"Thing-in-itself signifies that which exists independently of our perception by means of the senses. In other words, it is that which really and truly is. Democritus called this matter; in the end so did Locke; for Kant it was a x; and for me it is Will." *Parega and Paralipomena*

In Schopenhauer we see an effort, like Descartes, to establish a point of certainty. Rather than choosing a logical derivation as Descartes, Schopenhauer chose the will—what we also might loosely call desire. Schopenhauer is suggesting that this will exists a priori to reason. It is the "what is." Indeed, we all have a will or desire to live/survive. That important fact is often missed in purely logical analysis of things. But what is this will? Relative to the two-force model of man and woman balance, it is the will or desire to express our different sexualities (male individualization and female unification) for the purpose of our eternal procreation together. Schopenhauer's will is not so positive. His will was something like Freud's sexual unconsciousness; something that controlled us of which we could do little about. Schopenhauer saw the will to be blind, indifferent, and essentially overpowering to our lives. We are at the mercy of it. This was the basis of Schopenhauer's pessimism. He advocated a withdrawal from the world and perhaps a life of service to others (not dissimilar to Eastern religions) as the way to diminish the will's influence. I would submit to you that Schopenhauer's will is exactly that due to its one-force imbalance or, as he calls it, a thing-in-itself. Can you see this? Here is a perfect example of the mis-premise of philosophy—a singular force, i.e., "detached presence"—which has created the empiricist attack, undermining the whole idea of an absolute and leaving us frolicking in relativism.

John Stuart Mill (1806-1873)
"The object of this essay is to assert one very simple principle as entitled to govern absolutely the dealings of society with the individual in the way of compulsion and control, whether the means be physical force in the form of legal penalties, or the moral coercion of public opinion. That principle is, that the sole end for which mankind are warranted, individually or collectively, in interfering with the liberty of action of any of their number, is self-protection. The only purpose for which power can be rightfully exercised over any member of a civilized community, against his

will, is to prevent harm to others. His own good, either physical or moral, is not a sufficient warrant. He cannot rightfully be compelled to do or forbear because it will be better for him to do so, because it will make him happier, because, in the opinions of others, to do so would be wise, or even right." *On Liberty*

"If all mankind minus one were of one opinion, and only one person were of the contrary opinion, mankind would be no more justified in silencing that one person, than he, if he had the power, would be justified in silencing mankind." *On Liberty*

I have mixed feelings about J.S. Mill. Like Locke he was an empiricist. He expanded Locke's primary experience and attempted to show that logic itself was grounded not in innate ideas (universal axioms) but in experience/induction. This supposedly would give us direct linkage to logic, but unfortunately, it also took away the certainty of logic. It led Mill to the ethics of Utilitarianism. Utilitarianism is based on the idea of the greatest good for all. What exactly is this greatest good to be—based on what principle? Mill, in his writing *Principles of Political Economy*, essentially splits Capitalism in two. He agrees with the free market concerning the maximizing of production, but then turns around and suggests we need to control distribution. (Marxist thought seeks to control both aspects.) By what right does anyone have to control the production/distribution of another? The control of distribution very much fits into the ethics of Utilitarianism. Isn't the highest good where everyone gets to partake of everything? Says who? Having said this, I still like the above quotes from *On Liberty*. In the first quote, Mill gives to us the principle of the use of force—for self-defense. That, in essence, is the principle of the 2nd Amendment to the Constitution for the United States of America as well as the justification for the death penalty. We have a right to defend ourselves from aggresion. The second quote is one of my all-time favorites and is especially important today in light of the growing environment of political correctness with its corresponding "thought police" that is arising today over certain issues. It is becoming dangerous to take a stand, especially an absolute one.

Soren Kierkegaard (1813-1855)

"When we consider the question of truth in an objective manner, our thought is directed objectively to the truth, and this is considered as an object to which the thinker is related. However, our thought is not concentrated on the relationship but instead on the question of whether it is the truth to which the thinker is related. If the object to which he is related is the truth, he is reckoned to know the truth. When we consider the truth in a subjective manner, our thought is concentrated subjectively on the nature of our relationship (i.e., not on that to which it is related). If this relationship itself is a true one, we subjectively know the truth, even if the actual object of this relationship is untrue." *Concluding Unscientific Postscript*

A very interesting quote from Kierkegaard. What he is attempting to do, I believe, is give a deeper underpinning to life. Kierkegaard is considered to be the father of existentialism. Existentialism is known for the idea that existence is prior to essence or at least our focus ought to be on the human condition (the actual living of life) rather than on thought/logical systems. Kierkegaard's focus is on the individual and the subjective experience an individual has in life. He says that when our focus is objectively based we actually create a separation, focusing on the thought and thus disconnecting ourselves from the thing/another. We are not in the relationship as it were. As such we cut ourselves off from life and experience what he called dread. Kierkegaard would take his subjectivity and question anything even if it would take him to a place where he would conclude that the truth of a relationship at times overpowers the facts. It is, he would say, in this total surrender or leap of faith (of our objectivity) that we begin to experience the universal. I wonder if there really is such a split between the objective and the subjective. When we take a leap, don't we come down into something we again (logically) believe in? I would have to ask Kierkegaard if the 'spirit of the universal subjectivity' is more important than his Regine who he loved deeply but did not take in marriage. Make the right choice, my friend—that is the ultimate subjectivity (in more ways than one) in the facing of life head on.*

*Why must some of us, including myself, walk the lonely road when all we want or need is to give and receive love?

Karl Marx (1818-1884)
"The history of all hitherto existing society is the history of class struggles. The freeman and the slave, patrician and plebeian, pord and serf, guild-master and journeyman—in a word, the oppressor and the oppressed, in constant opposition to one another, have carried on an uninterrupted, sometimes hidden, sometimes open conflict, a conflict that each time ended either in a revolutionary reconstitution of the entire society or the common ruin of the conflicting classes.... The modern bourgeois society which has sprung up from the ruins of feudal society has not done away with class conflicts. It has only established new classes, new conditions of oppression, new forms of conflict in place of the old ones." *Communist Manifesto*

"From each according to his abilities, to each according to his needs." *Critique of the Gotha Program*

Marx, of course, is known as the father of communism. It is not difficult to understand his thought if we return to Hegel. He used Hegel's dialectic process (thesis—anti-thesis—synthesis) but instead of relating it to some Absolute Spirit, related it to the course of materialism, i.e., our survival on this planet. Marx suggested that it was the material conditions of life that created our consciousness not the other way around. He had a further interesting point that the world "out there" was not just to be discovered but directed. In other words, the world "out there" is affected by our perception of it just as we are affected by the world. This, actually, is the essence of relationship. Unfortunately for Marx, his concept of a relationship always seemed to be affected by class struggle and conflict (the imbalanced teeter-totter). He did not understand the metaphysical balance in play. Thus, he was led down the path of attempting to develop a politics and economics that appeared to represent everyone (the people) but actually represented no one. His famous quote—*From each according to his abilities, to each according to his needs*—

pretty much says it all. (Following Descartes' Cogito—*I think, therefore I am*—the "New Age" Marxists would say, *I feel, therefore I deserve*.) It is this exact economic equation that ensures class struggle, victimhood/envy, and our inability to survive. All systems that base their economies on that statement fail. Interesting enough, that doesn't seem to detour too many in the one-force paradigm.

Friedrich Nietzsche (1844-1900)

"The 'thing-in-itself' is a nonsensical concept. If I remove all the relationships, all the 'properties,' all the 'activities' of a thing, nothing remains. Thingness has only been invented by us to fit the requirements of logic. In other words, with the aim of defining, of communication. (In order to bind together the multiplicity of relationships, properties, and activities.)" *Will to Power*

"We cannot both affirm and deny the same thing. This is a subjective empirical law—nothing to do with logical "necessity," only of our inability to do it…. In Aristotle's view, the law of contradiction is the most certain basic principle of them all. It is the ultimate and most fundamental principle upon which all demonstrative proof rests. The principles of every axiom depend upon it. Yet if this is really the case, we should perhaps examine more thoroughly what *presuppositions* are already involved here. Either it says something about actuality, about being, as if we already knew it from another source; that is, as if opposite attributes could not be ascribed to it. Or it means: opposite attributes should not be ascribed to it. In which case, logic would not be an imperative to know the truth, as formerly supposed, but merely an imperative to organize a world that we could look upon as the true one…. Thus it remains an open question—Do the axioms of logic precisely match reality? Or are they simply a means and method for us to *create* a concept of "reality" that suits us? As already indicated, to agree with the first question we would have to possess a previous knowledge of being (i.e., one prior to our use of, and in no way involved with, logic). And this is certainly not the case. The proposition (the one that forms the law of contradiction) thus involves no criteria of truth. It is simply an *imperative* saying what should count as true." *Will to Power*

"I have never yet found a woman with whom I should like to have children, unless it be this woman who I love: for I love thee, O Eternity! For I love thee, O Eternity!" *Thus Spoke Zarathustra LX, The Seven Seals*

Nietzsche is one of the most profound philosophers. He certainly was a philosophical revolutionary. I credit him with at least cracking the one-force paradigm. In the first quote by him we note that he saw a flaw in the idea of a thing-in-itself, the one-force detached "presence." His famous quote that "God is dead," essentially suggested that the idea of a singular metaphysical force (that is beyond our knowing) is no longer applicable to our lives. He saw man (men and women) as a creator. This was the idea behind his "will to power." We are creators, not just beings at the mercy of some grand creator. Now, in the second quote by him, we begin to enter into dangerous ground. He is questioning the axioms of logic—do they only serve as a means and method for us to *create* a concept of "reality" that suits us? "There are no facts, only interpretations," he would say. In other words, is creation an open field, i.e., can we create anything we want? In today's parlance we would ask, do we create our own reality or is there an (absolute) reality from which we can then create? Is there an ultimate reality (objective and independent) which we must adhere to whereby we may live and create, or is reality only of our making and experience without any metaphysical, epistemological, or ethical limits? What Nietzsche failed to see was his own presuppositions. He is assuming that we can *create* without looking at the metaphysical ramifications of that idea. Perhaps the process of creation is itself a logical and absolute process. Perhaps our ability to create is due to the fact there is a creative process. To suggest that consciousness is conceptual is also to suggest that consciousness is a creative process (based on the law of opposites in balance) but creative only within the limits of that process. Nietzsche is a perfect example of the problem in philosophy. He himself sees the one-force misconception of historical rationalism but his solution denies truth altogether. From this point, whether one goes down the empiricist track or the existentialist track, it does not matter. The end result is a deconstruction of truth, the blind belief in no limits, the relativity of anything goes. I believe Nietzsche was close though. We can see that in the last quote. *...for I love thee, O Eternity!*

John Dewey (1859-1952)
"If the term 'matter' is given a philosophic interpretation, over and above its technical scientific meaning—e.g., *mass* until recently—this meaning, I believe, should be to name a functional relation rather than a substance." *Experience, Knowledge and Value*

"To assume that anything can be known in isolation from its connections with other things is to identify knowing with merely having some object before perception or in feeling, and is thus to lose the key to the traits that distinguish an object as known....The more connections and interactions we ascertain the more we *know* the object in question." *The Later Works, 1925-1953*

"Democracy is possible only because of a change in intellectual conditions. It implies tools for getting at truth in detail, and day by day, as we go along. Only such possession justifies the surrender of fixed, all-embracing principles to which, as universals, all particulars and individuals are subject for valuation and regulation." *The Structure of Experience*

Dewey completes the Pragmatists track begun by Charles Sanders Peirce (1839-1914) and William James. Pragmatism is an American version of empiricism. Now, if you look at the above quotes in terms of the one-force misconception, i.e., the "detached presence," I tend to agree with Dewey. In other words, let's not just view matter as a thing-in-itself but relationally. Nothing is of itself alone. For example, we can't just study maleness. Maleness is always in contrast to femaleness. So we ought to study both. That is what Dewey is suggesting in the second quote. In essence, there is no isolated ultimate reality. This was the idea behind Dewey's instrumental logic that was concerned with the *function* of things. Pragmatism has to do with the functionality of things, does something work or not. But I guess we cannot ask why something works for that would, at the very least, imply a universal working or order to things. In Dewey's functionalism ultimate truth was not necessary. Study the thing in its function; that is all. Truth is not fixed per se, we "get at it." But how? What is the basis/principles such that we can know anything about anything? The problem I have with Pragmatism is that it never comes to an answer; the facts are never in. Metaphysically, Pragmatism is another form of relativism.

Bertrand Russell (1872-1970)

"At the age of eleven, I began Euclid, with my brother as my tutor. This was one of the great events of my life, as dazzling as first love. I had not imagined that there was anything so delicious in the world. After I had learned the fifth proposition, my brother told me that it was generally considered difficult, but I had found no difficulty whatsoever. This was the first time it had dawned upon me that I might have some intelligence. From that moment until Whitehead and I finished *Principia Mathematica*, when I was thirty-eight, mathematics was my chief interest, and my chief source of happiness. Like all happiness, however, it was not unalloyed. I had been told that Euclid proved things, and was much disappointed that he started with axioms. At first I refused to accept them unless my brother could offer me some reason for doing so, but he said: 'If you don't accept them we cannot go on,' and as I wished to go on, I reluctantly admitted them *pro tem*. The doubt as to the premises of mathematics which I felt at that moment remained with me, and determined the course of my subsequent work." *The Autobiography of Bertrand Russell, 1872 – 1912*

"Philosophy is to be studied, not for the sake of any definite answers to its questions, since no definite answers can, as a rule, be known to be true, but rather for the sake of the questions themselves; because these questions enlarge our conception of what is possible, enrich our intellectual imagination and diminish the dogmatic assurance which close the mind against speculation; but above all because, through the greatness of the universe which philosophy contemplates, the mind also is rendered great, and becomes capable of that union with the universe which constitutes its highest good." *The Problems of Philosophy*

Bertrand Russell was one of the great logicians of our times. He, along with Alfred North Whitehead, wrote the immense work *Principia Mathematica*. What Russell sought to do was to give mathematics a logical basis that would be the most precise and certain knowledge there is. You can see in the first quote above Russell's enthusiasm in the logical form of Euclidean geometry. But he couldn't quite get over the idea that Euclid began his geometry from certain (non-provable) axioms. How could that be? Certainly, there must be a logical basis for axioms. This was Russell's quest in attempting to give a logical basis to mathematics. Unfortunately for him, he ran into various walls or paradoxes which led him to the conclusion that mathematics does not necessarily reduce to logic; that its logic arises from its (non-provable) axioms. Wow! We see the disappointment in Russell in the second quote. Later there was an Austrian mathematician named Kurt Godel (1906-1978) who was to show that any system, such as mathematics, would contain some propositions that could not be proved within the system. In other words, there must be a given to things. The given itself is non-provable but is itself the basis of all proof (logic). I mean, why the two (equal and opposite) forces? There is no answer to that other than because that is life. Life is why? Life will have to do.

In the last quote by Russell, we see what philosophy is today—"for the sake of the questions." Just like the quote by Paul Strathern that led off this addendum, so philosophy has given up. It, too, has been reduced to relativity.

Martin Heidegger (1889-1976)
"Philosophy remains latent in every human existence and need not be first added to it from somewhere else." *The Metaphysical Foundations of Logic*

"Philosophy gets under way only by a peculiar insertion of our own existence into the fundamental possibilities of Dasein as a whole. For this insertion three things are of decisive importance. First, we must allow space for beings as a whole. Second, we must release ourselves into the nothing: in other words, we must liberate ourselves from those idols everyone has before which everyone cringes. And finally, we must let the sweep of our suspense take its full course so that it swings back into the basic question of metaphysics which the nothing itself compels: why is there being at all, and why not rather nothing?" *What Is Metaphysics?*

The focus of Heidegger's thought was on being. What does it mean to be in the world? You might say he sought a pure experience of being. Heidegger was influenced by the phenomenology of Husserl (1859-1938) who sought to achieve a pure consciousness— our primal given-ness or transcendental self. Heidegger saw the concept of being as more primary than consciousness but the idea that we ought to get down to the essential remains the same. Heidegger thought that the whole intellectual journey beginning with Socrates to discover the "what is" had been in vain. That intellectualism had missed the primary of our beingness. We have lost, or never found, the primeval experience of ourselves. Kierkegaard was about this as well. We must reach beyond (or behind) the logic/reasoning of our minds and find who we really are. Or, as Heidegger would say, we must release ourselves into the nothingness and let go of all our preconceptions to truly experience ourselves. Heidegger is speaking to something more fundamental than Descartes' *Cogito* (I think, therefore I am.) He viewed Descartes as trapped in a "languaging of reason" that prevented him from really "letting go" into the nothingness. Now, this is all well and good except for the concept/experience of being itself. There isn't any being-in-itself. There are sexual beings, male and female. Perhaps we ought to actually experience the *metaphysical* nature of our sexual beings in relation to our sexual opposite. Now that would be an experience, don't you think? And to do this, we need not lose the logic of sexual polarity itself. Rather we need to understand it to thereby surrender to our sexual other half in the eternal relationship that we together comprise.

Ludwig Wittgenstein (1889-1951)

"In logic nothing is accidental: if a thing *can* occur in a state of affairs, the possibility of the state of affairs must be written into the thing itself." *Tractatus Logico-Philosophicus*

"The correct method in philosophy would really be the following: to say nothing except what can be said, i.e., propositions of natural science—i.e., something that has nothing to do with philosophy—and then, whenever someone else wanted to say something metaphysical to demonstrate to him that he had failed to give a meaning to certain signs in his proposition." *Tractatus Logico-Philosophicus*

"Philosophy may in no way interfere with the actual use of language; it can in the end only describe it. For it cannot give it any foundation either. It leaves everything as it is…." *Philosophical Investigations*

"It is the business of philosophy not to resolve a contradiction by means of a mathematical or logic-mathematical discovery, but to make it possible for us to get a clear view of the state of…affairs before the contradiction is resolved." *Philosophical Investigations*

Wittgenstein is an interesting philosopher. I won't say he was an empiricist in that he sought to base knowledge not in experience per se but in logic. Like Russell, he wanted to discover the logical foundations of mathematics, and even more than that, discover the foundations of logic itself. Yet, I don't know that he was a rationalist in that he saw philosophy as descriptive rather than deductive and as completely doing away with metaphysics. He viewed the task of philosophy as being the study of language. "A is the same as the letter A," he would say. Further, the limits of language are the limits of thought. "What we cannot speak upon let us then be silent." I believe he is referring to "metaphysics" concerning the one-force, non-relational, thing-in-itself "detached presence." Yet, what does Wittgenstein leave us with? Well, the one idea I take from him is that propositions and reality have the same logical form. But what is this form? We are back to the question, what are the foundations of logic itself? I would suggest to you that it is the distinction between a one order and a two forces (equal and opposite) bringing forth Aristotle's Laws of Logic Revised (and Sexed). You see, our initial axiom(s) must be procreative: a *two forces* or said in more specific terms—*it takes a man and a woman to make a baby*. Has philosophy failed us in not incorporating the procreative process of life itself into its study? You decide.

Jean-Paul Sartre (1905-1980)

"Man is condemned to be free." *Existentialism and Humanism*

"The world of explanations and reason is not that of existence." *Nausea*

"The essential thing is contingency. In other words, by logical definition, existence is not necessity. To exist just means *to be there*; what exists simply appears and lets itself be encountered. You can never deduce it." *Nausea*

"The first effect of existentialism is that it puts every man in possession of himself as he is, and places the entire responsibility of his existence upon his own shoulders." *Existentialism and Humanism*

"Atheistic existentialism, of which I am a representative, maintains that if God doesn't exist there is at least one being whose existence comes before its essence—that is, a being which exists before it can be defined by any conception of it. That being is man—or, as Heidegger calls it, human reality…. Man first of all exists, encounters himself, surges up in the world—and defines himself afterwards…. Man is not definable, because to begin with he is nothing. He will not be anything until later, and then he will be what he makes himself." *Existentialism and Humanism*

"Consciousness is complete emptiness (because the entire world is outside it)." *Being and Nothingness*

"Hell is other people." *In Camera*

In Sartre we have the quintessential existentialist. What I like about Sartre and his existentialism is the level of personal responsibility required. Our existence is placed upon our own shoulders as he would say. No one else is going to make our lives for us. Taken to its logical conclusion, Sartre would say, in effect, there isn't any "God" to save us. Existentialism does take away the "detached presence" but it does so at the cost of metaphysics itself. What is the ultimate order or reality? Well, there isn't one. (The essential thing is contingency not necessity.) What is to be the basis of our reason? Who knows? Do we have an essential (sexual) essence as man and woman balance suggests. No, we become what we create ourselves to be. Sartre, like Nietzsche, presupposes a creative process without looking at the metaphysical ramifications of that fact of reality. Maybe this creative, or shall I say, *procreative* process, is absolutely exact in its nature, logical in it form, and universal in is presence. Existentialism has reverted to the anything goes relativism of today exactly because it did not have an *absolute* to base itself upon.

Jacques Derrida (1930-2004)
"What is neither true nor false is reality. But as soon as speech is inaugurated, one is in the register of the unveiling of the truth as of its contract of properness: presence, speech, testimony."
The Post Card: From Socrates to Freud and Beyond

"When I speak, I am conscious of being present for what I think, but also of keeping as close as possible to my thought a signifying substance, a sound carried by my breath." JD

"All attempts to define deconstruction are bound to be false.... One of the principal things in deconstruction is the delimiting of ontology and above all of the third person present indicative: propositions of the form 'S is P.'" JD

If Sartre's existentialism/relativity is credited with finishing off philosophy, or at least the metaphysics/absolutes, maybe we should pause and rather give that "honor" to Derrida. Derrida argued that all of philosophy was based on what he calls an *aporia* ("detached presence"). He would say that absolute truth can only be guaranteed by a "detached presence" which in itself defeats the quest for absolute truth. Therefore, the whole basis of philosophy since Socrates in the quest for truth/reason is flawed. Derrida called his "philosophy" deconstructionism. He sought to deconstruct philosophy and language itself of this *aporia* implication that he claims has controlled our thought from the beginning. Language should never presume or strive to express a metaphysical assumption or essence to things. There isn't any absolute truth, not even in logic, and so we ought not base our lives upon that idea. Well, what is there then? According to Derrida, there is our consciousness which somehow exists beyond or prior to logic/reasoning and which does not intuit a "detached presence." I think this is something like Heidegger's "being" or even the empiricist's "pure experience." There must be some "pure" experience that takes us beyond the rigors of absolute conception/ survival, mustn't there? (It is interesting to see so many philosophers so desperately seeking something beyond the reason of non-contradictory logic and, when they supposedly find it, want it to have all the certainty of reality as if it was based on non-contradictory logic!) Anyway, Derrida leaves us with language as our vehicle of experience/expression, a language free of any absolute basis of determining its meaning. Language is to be relative—having many meanings or different meanings for different people. Like cultural relativism, we now have language relativism. This actually leads to mental chaos. Yet, I do agree with Derrida's point about philosophy being permeated with a "detached presence." That is what I call the one-force misconception. But the answer is not to "deconstruct" the ideas of an absolute truth, logic, and reason altogether but to correct the mis-premise. Correct the mis-premise and we will see the chasm between consciousness and existence disappear. *Consciousness is an order of two sexual forces.*

Paul-Michel Foucault (1926-1984)

"Each society had its regime of truth, its 'general politics' of truth: that is, the types of discourse which it accepts and makes junction as true." *P-MF*

"What I meant was that I think what the gay movement needs now is much more the art of life than a science or scientific knowledge (or pseudoscientific knowledge) of what sexuality is. Sexuality is a part of our behavior. It's a part of our world freedom. Sexuality is something that we ourselves create—it is our own creation, and much more than the discovery of a secret side of our desire. We have to understand that with our desires, through our desires, go new forms of relationships, new forms of love, new forms of creation. Sex is not a fatality: it's a possibility for creative life." *Ethics: Subjectivity and Truth*

"Yes. You see, if there was no resistance, there would be no power relations. Because it would simply be a matter of obedience. You have to use power relations to refer to the situation where you're not doing what you want. So resistance comes first, and resistance remains superior to the forces of the process; power relations are obliged to change with the resistance. So I think that *resistance* is the main word, *the key word*, in this dynamic." *Ethics: Subjectivity and Truth*

"I should say, also, that I think that in the lesbian movement, the fact that women have been, for centuries and centuries, isolated in society, frustrated, despised in many ways, and so on, has given them the real possibility of constituting a society, of creating a kind of social relation between themselves, outside the social world that was dominated by males. Lillian Faderman's book *Surpassing the Love of Men* is very interesting in this regard. It raises the question: What kind of emotional experience, what kind of relationships, were possible in a world where women in society had no social, no legal, and no political power? And she argues that women used that isolation and lack of power." *Ethics: Subjectivity and Truth*

In Foucault we see the perfect example of the "philosophy" of relativism. This is not to suggest that Foucault did not have some interesting things to say. In his writing *Civilization and Madness*, Foucault suggests that reason (like Descartes *Cogito*) did not take us deep enough into our own madness (or nothingness as Heidegger would say). (Perhaps reason/logic/ conception does not give to us the quintessential experience of life but at least it gives to us the vehicle to give meaning to such an experience when we have it.) In another writing, *The Order of Things: An Archaeology of the Human Sciences*, Foucault brings forth the idea of an *episteme* which means the structure of a given thought, its presuppositions, assumptions, and even prejudices that affect it. Foucault would suggest to Derrida, I think, that an *aporia* ("detached presence") is a part of the episteme of what makes up (or had made up) philosophy. Every thought system or culture is made up of certain epistemes, i.e., belief systems, mind-sets, or paradigms that define that thought or culture. This is interesting but why can't the actual truth be our "episteme"? Foucault's episteme is like Kant's categories. It gives to us the impression that we can never know the "real truth" behind the world of appearances or paradigms. Foucault was highly influenced by Nietzsche's ideas of man as creator and the will to power. He was also an existentialist holding that existence is primary to essence. In other words, it is suggested, we create our own realities in a world of no ultimate reality or limits. We see in the quotes above that, according to Foucult, even our sexuality was something to be created. In other words, there aren't any metaphysical constraints to it. Gay, straight, bisexual, transgender, all these are just expressions of who one "really" is. Expression becomes the new "God." *Relativity rules*. Foucault focuses on power relations (the imbalanced teeter-tooter) and the use of resistance (like Marx's class struggle) against those who might attempt to deny another's "self-expression." This is exactly the modus operandi of the gay movement today. Express/resist. "You cannot define me because there aren't any absolute definitions." But there are—life itself and its procreative process. Foucault actually is the perfect expression of the result of what happens when philosophy (and all life) collapses into (gender) relativism. *Relativity destroys all that it touches.* All of philosophy (and life) collapses into a denial of the process of life and a resistance to any suggestion that there actually is a metaphysical given such as two (equal and opposite) forces, i.e., procreative love. What a contradiction.

Ayn Rand (1905-1982)

"Any theory that propounds an opposition between the logical and the empirical represents a failure to grasp the nature of logic and its role in human cognition. Man's knowledge is not acquired by logic apart from experience or by experience apart from logic, *but by the application of logic to experience*. All truths are the product of a logical identification of the fact of experience." *Introduction to Objectivist Epistemology*

"Axioms are usually considered to be propositions identifying a fundamental, self-evident truth. But explicit propositions as such are not primaries: they are made of concepts. The base of man's knowledge—of all other concepts, all axioms, propositions and thought—consists of axiomatic concepts…. An axiomatic concept is the identification of a primary fact of reality, which cannot be analyzed, i.e., reduced to other facts or broken into component parts. It is implicit in all facts and in all knowledge. It is fundamentally given and directly perceived or experienced, which requires no proof or explanation, but on which all proofs and explanations rest…. The first and primary axiomatic concepts are "existence," "identity" (which is a corollary of "existence") and "consciousness." One can study what exists and how consciousness functions; but one cannot analyze (or "prove") existence as such, or consciousness as such. These are irreducible primaries. (An attempt to "prove" them is self-contradictory: it is an attempt to "prove" existence by means of non-existence, and consciousness by means of unconsciousness.)" *Introduction to Objectivist Epistemology*

"The act of isolation involved (in concept-formation) is a process of *abstraction*: i.e., a selective mental focus that *takes out* or separates a certain aspect of reality from all others (e.g., isolates a certain attribute from the entities possessing it, or a certain action from the entities performing it, etc.)" *Introduction to Objectivist Epistemology*

"Metaphysics—the science that deals with the fundamental nature of reality—involves man's widest abstractions. It includes every concrete he has ever perceived; it involves such a vast sum of knowledge and such a long chain of concepts that no man could hold it all in the focus of his immediate consciousness awareness. Yet he needs that sum and that awareness to guide him—he needs the power to summon them into full conscious focus…. That power is given to him by art." *The Romantic Manifesto*

"Aristotle's philosophy was the intellect's Declaration of Independence. Aristotle, the father of logic, should be given the title of the world's first intellectual, in the purest and noblest sense of that word. No matter what remnants of Platonism did exist in Aristotle's system, his incomparable achievement lay in the fact that he defined the *basic* principles of a rational view of existence and of man's consciousness: that there is only *one* reality; the one which man perceives—that it exists as an *objective* absolute (which means: independently of the consciousness, the wishes or the feelings of any perceiver)—that the task of man's consciousness is to *perceive*, not to create, reality—that abstractions are man's method of integrating his sensory material—that man's mind is his only tool of knowledge—that A is A…. If we consider the fact that to this day everything that makes us civilized beings, every rational value that we possess—including the birth of science, the industrial revolution, the creation of the United States, even the structure of our language—is the result of Aristotle's influence, of the degree to which, explicitly or implicitly, men accepted his epistemological principles, we would have to say: never have so many owed so much to one man." *For the New Intellectual*

"She felt—as she had felt it one spring night, slumped across her desk in the crumbing office of the John Galt Line, by a window facing a dark alley—the sense and vision of her own world, which she would never reach…. You—she thought—whomever you are, whom I have always loved and never found, you whom I expected to see at the end of the rails beyond the horizon, you whose presence I had always felt in the streets of the city and whose world I had wanted to build, it is my love for you that had kept me moving, my love and my hope to reach you and my wish to be worthy of you on the day when I would stand before you face to face. Now I know that I shall never find you—that it is not to be reached or lived—but what is left of my life is still yours, and I will go on in your name, even though it is a name I'll never learn, I will go on serving you, even though I'm never to win, I will go on. To be worthy of you on the day when I would have met you, even though I won't.... She had never accepted hopelessness, but she stood at the window and, addressed to the shape of a fog bound city, it was her self-dedication to unrequited love." *Atlas Shrugged*

"Dagny...I had seen...what it was that I had to fight for...I had to save you...not to let you stumble the years of your life away, struggling on through a poisoned fog...struggling to find, at the end of your road, not the towers of a city, but a fat, soggy, mindless cripple performing his enjoyment of life by means of swallowing the gin *your* life had gone to pay for!" *Atlas Shrugged*

Did Ayn Rand make the *procreant touch* that I am speaking of? Well, let me just say, Ayn Rand was the one philosopher who, post Aristotle, came the closest to putting it all together. She understood that consciousness was conceptual. Look at her quote where she unifies the discrepancy between logic and experience, or the quote when she speaks of axiomatic concepts as self-evident, and so on. I don't have to say much about her quotes as they are so clear. Ayn Rand had a thorough understanding of both epistemology and metaphysics. And do you know what? She was only a novelist. Perhaps that is why philosophy (what's left of it) refuses to take her seriously. Shouldn't she be honored as the world's greatest philosopher? Well, perhaps not. We see her limitation in her metaphysical primary that A is A (existence exists). Where is B? Apparently, she, too, did not bring forth the *opposite other* as also being primary in her philosophy. Her epistemology, like Aristotle's, is a two-way process. Her metaphysics though is still one force, singular in its inception. How unfortunate. So close. In the next to last quote above, we see Dagny Taggart, the heroine of her great novel *Atlas Shrugged*, speak out for her eternal love. "You... whomever you are, whom I have always loved and never found,...you whose presence I had always felt...,it is my love for you that had kept me moving, my love and my hope to reach you and my wish to be worthy of you on the day when I would stand before you face to face...but what is left of my life is still yours, and I will go on in your name, even though it is a name I'll never learn, I will go on serving you, even though I'm never to win, I will go on."

Don't we all feel this sense of eternal love in our hearts? Ayn Rand didn't find it in this world—but she sure must have felt it. Perhaps her one-force metaphysic prevented that. But we **together** can find it. We can know the eternal in the two-force paradigm of man and woman balance. Ayn Rand apparently did not equate the procreative as axiomatic (self-evident) to life, that the conceptual and the procreative were one and the same process. Her metaphysics did not take her to the necessity of procreation, **of child**. But ours does. The eternal lies in our children. This is what I have so needed for us to understand—*our children*—to save not just ourselves but our children from the poisoned fog of (LGBTQ) relativity. No philosopher to date has seen what is so obvious. I guess they have been too busy looking for the "thing-in-itself" or the "pure experience" or the "essential life" or "my way," to recognize the smile on the face of the child most of them never had. And it is a mystery in a way, the most important thing in life, man and woman balance/procreation, has not been equated as primary to life. Well, let me suggest that it is—big time!

To conclude this Investigation, let us review some quotations from the writings of Walter and Lao Russell. I hope you can see the philosophical leap they made. They opened the door to a *procreant universe*. They give **LIFE** to our fundamental metaphysics. Now we can know that philosophy has an absolute metaphysical base. It is our *procreative love*. Not my procreative love; not your procreative love. No, *our* procreative love. Can you see this? **We cannot procreate by ourselves alone.** And yet, as you read through the following quotes, notice the difficulty even the Russell's had in surmising the fundamental principle of life, is it "the One," or is it "the Two"? Let's proceed.

Walter Russell (1871-1963)
"In the beginning, God. There is but one God. There is but one

universe. God is the universe. God is not one and the universe another. The universe is not a separate creation of God's. It is God. There is no created universe. Nothing is which has not always been... Man conceives a perfect and omnipotent God. A perfect and omnipotent God could not create imperfection. He could not create a lesser than Himself. He could not create a greater than Himself. God could not create other than Himself. God did not create other than Himself, nor greater, nor lesser than Himself."
The Universal One

"Light as man knows light, is but an unstable simulation of the real light of the Universal One. Man's concept of light is luminosity, an illusion of the universal light of inertia, sustained in its appearance as an illusion of light by the pressures generated through motion. The inner mind of ecstatic man knows the real light and that he is One with light. He is not deceived by its illusion."
The Universal One

"Light as man knows light, is but an unstable simulation of the real light of the Universal One. Man's concept of light is luminosity, an illusion of the universal light of inertia, sustained in its appearance as an illusion of light by the pressures generated through motion. The inner mind of ecstatic man knows the real light and that he is One with light. He is not deceived by its illusion."
The Universal One

"All idea, and all forms of idea are the result of union between equal or unequal opposite actions and reactions of force. Perfection of mating lies in the union of exactly equal and opposite male actions and female reactions. In perfection of union lies stability. Imperfection of union lies instability. Unequal actions and reactions will unite with unwillingness which increases in proportion to their degree of departure from exact equality in opposition. When the potentials of the opposites are too far removed from equality, then will union cease. In organic life the union or reproduction of opposites is limited, and beyond the limitations, reproduction is impossible. In the chemistry of inorganic life, the unstable union of unequal opposite states of motion is also limited, and beyond the limitations union and reproduction is impossible. This is a universe of reproduction of idea in accumulated potential of the constant of energy, of registration of the soul of idea in inertia, and of reproduction of accumulated potential.

"Unions of opposed actions and reactions are possible only within certain limitations. When union does not take place there can be no reproduction. Equal and opposite actions and reactions, when united, are satisfied in their unions and will remain united. Stable unions will always reproduce true to species. Unequal and opposite actions and reactions, when united, are unsatisfied in their unions and will always seek their true tonal mates. Unsatisfied unions are unstable unions. Unstable unions never reproduce true to species. Unstable unions tend to return to their separate tonal states. If either mate in an unstable union finds a more equal mate, it will always leave the former and go to the latter." *The Universal One*

"The entire 'created universe' of all that is, ever has been, or ever will be, is but the One substance in motion, light. God is light and in Him is no darkness at all. (John1-5) Matter is light. God and matter are One. Spirit and matter are the same substance. That substance is light. There are not two substances in the universe. There cannot be two substances in the universe. The substance of the universal Mind is a living substance. That which man calls life is an inherent property of the entirety of Mind. Light is life. There is but One Life in the Universe. The whole of the universe is but one living, breathing, pulsing Being. There are not two lives or two living beings in the universe. There are not two of anything in the universe. The universe and all that is, is One." *The Universal One*

"God is not one and the universe another. The Universe is not a separate creation of God's. It is God. There is no created-universe. Nothing is which has not always been…. This is a 'creating' universe, not a 'created' one." *The Universal One*

" …Sex is the great third principle. Sex is the controlling cause of both force and motion. Without it, neither could continue….Sex is the motive power behind force and motion. Sex is the apparent division of the father-mother substance of mind into apparent opposites…Sex is the active desire of Mind for division into opposites, and its reactive desire for unity. Sex is that motive force which demands separability into two, and equally desires union of the apparent two into one. Mind, being One, cannot yield to the desire of Mind for separation into two. Sex desire of Mind for divisibility into two succeeds only in producing an appearance of divisibility into two. Likewise, sex desire of Mind for unity into One succeeds only in reproducing an apparent composite of the two. Sex is of all things from the beginning. Sex begins when light begins. Sex is the desire for the appearance of being which constitutes the appearance of existence. Nothing can be without the desire to be. All things are which desire to be. Desire dominates all thinking. Desire dominates all matter. All desire is sex desire." *The Universal One*

"That which is produced must be reproduced. No state of motion ever ends. All states of motion are forever reproduced. All states of motion of apparently separate things are actions and reactions of the force which produced them. All varying idea of Mind is registered in separate states of motion which have measurable dimensions. The reproduction of all idea is the result of union of the action and reaction which register that idea. Every action is male. Every reaction is female. Every action is electro-positive. Every rection is electro-negative. Every action has its equal and opposite reaction. Every action and every reaction is a tone in an octave of the universal constant of energy. Equal and opposite actions and reactions, when united, comprise a unit of an octave of the universal constant of energy. An action and its opposite reaction are not two Their energies, when combined, make one. Reaction is born of action; and action is born again of reaction." *The Universal One*

"For again I say My one principle of My one law is founded upon the solid rock of equal interchange between all pairs of opposite things, opposite conditions, or opposite transactions between men." *The Divine Iliad*

"For My universe is but the forever unfolding-refolding of My One Whole Idea. As My Whole Idea is perfect, so, also, is each part perfect." *The Divine Iliad*

"The Father-Mother of Creation divides His sexless unity into sex-divided pairs of father and mother bodies, for the purpose of uniting them to create other pairs of father and mother bodies in eternal sequences forever." *Atomic Suicide?**

**Atomic Suicide?* was co-authored by both Walter and Lao Russell.

"God, the creator, divides His one white Light by extending its ONENESS into electrical tensions of vibrating red and blue pairs. The tensions of this electrical division are equaled by a desire for unity, which is attained at the point of white incandescence in matter. Unity thus attained is repeated forever by the same dividing, uniting process of electrical action-reaction pulsations. Reproduction cannot take place until the red and blue lights of sex-divided motion are voided in the still White Light of the Creator. Man alone, of all Creation, ever knows of his Omniscience." *Atomic Suicide?*

"Mankind has thought of sex in terms of a relation between the opposite sexes in organic living systems, never for a moment including sex relations in the mineral kingdom, in hot suns, or the ice caps of the poles of planets. We have used such terms as cohabitation and sex relation as though the sex relation is entirely separate and apart from other relations, and as though its reproductive effect is limited to living things that die or decay.

"From now on, sex will be regarded in our new perspective as being expressed continuously and perpetually in all things. Instead of thinking in terms of cohabitation and human sexual relationships, sex should be thought of as the interchange between pairs of oppositely unbalanced conditions for the purpose of balancing these conditions in every effect of motion in the entire universe. 'Good effects' are those in which the interchange is balanced--and 'bad effects' are those in which balance is not complete." *Home Study Course in Universal Law, Natural Science, and Living Philosophy*—co-authored by both Walter and Lao Russell.

"Man cannot conceive any possible mechanical device or principle which will perform work, store energy, or transmit power, which is not founded upon the alternating compression-expansion sequences of universal inbreathings and outbreathings."*

*Not sure from which writing of Dr. Russell's this quote is from.

Lao Russell (1904-1988)

"Know thou that thou shalt know space, but never emptiness for:

"Behold! I am Space and I fill all of it.

"I am its One, its undivided Father-Mother One of my universe.

"I divide My oneness, and behold! I am two—father and mother.

"These two extend from Me, one on My right hand and one on My left.

"Each equally balanced with the other in the Oneness of their matehood.

"And then, behold! My two become one in Me, the One Father-Mother, undivided—To again become two to Father-Mother my eternal universe." *Why You Cannot Die: The Continuity of Life, Reincarnation Explained*

Let's us quickly analyze. Dr. Russell states: *"There is but One Life in the Universe. The whole of the universe is but one living, breathing, pulsing Being. There are not two lives or two living beings in the universe. There are not two of anything in the universe. The universe and all that is, is One."* He also states: *"The Father-Mother of Creation divides His sexless unity into sex-divided pairs of father and mother bodies, for the purpose of uniting them to create other pairs of father and mother bodies in eternal sequences forever."* What is the Metaphysical Absolute if you will? Is the Father-Mother of Creation the One Order? Certainly, there must be a **living process** included. And what is the sexless unity? Is that the fundamental or is the "sexless unity" and the sex-divided pairs that comprise the one order/process? I would like to suggest that the whole "sexless unity" and the sex-divided pairs constitute the one order/process of the universe and that its fundamental nature is sexual. The sexual process itself is one of Division and Unification. The "sexless unity" is not fundamental nor is it sexless. There isn't a sexless point if you will that exists prior to or apart from the whole sexual process of male and female division and unification. Unity or unification does not exist outside of or prior to the sexual process but is but one half of the sexual process. Just like breathing—there is inhalation and exhalation. Neither come first. Both come together. And there isn't any existence prior to or in back of inhalation and exhalation. In other words, there isn't an intermediary between inhalation or exhalation; there isn't an intermediary between male and female. They come together or they don't come at all.

Now look at Lao Russell's quote. I think she is a little more precise in her languaging between the **One** and the **Two**. *"And then, behold! My two become one in Me, the One Father-Mother, undivided—To again become two to Father-Mother my eternal universe."* Not so easy; the answer to this lies in the comprehension of a **Life Procreant Process—the One and the Two come together or they do not come at all!**

If I may I would like to turn your attention to my friend Robert Birk who I have dedicated this writing to. I remember the day well when I was introduced to the writings of Walter Russell. It was through Robert. Robert and I first met at Southern Oregon College in Ashland, Oregon, 1968. We became good friends. In my second year of college, we roomed together. Robert took the winter term off and was living in Portland. I was on the SOC swim team. We had an upcoming meet in Portland. I contacted Robert to see if he could come to the meet so we could visit. He did. He brought a book with him. The book was *The Man Who Tapped the Secrets of the Universe* by Glenn Clark, 1946. Robert told me that he had just read the book and suggested I give it a read. He said that he had come across a passage in the book that touched him deeply. As the meet was two days, I was able to read the book that evening. Robert came back to the meet the next day. I told him I, too, was touched by the book. I pointed to a passage in the book. Glenn Clark is interviewing Walter Russell.

Glenn Clark (1882-1956)—*The Man Who Tapped the Secrets of the Universe*, 1946

Glenn Clark: "You say you never studied physics and have read but few books in your life. Tell me how you acquired your scientific knowledge."

Dr. Russell: "It is because I always looked for the CAUSE behind things and didn't fritter away my time analyzing EFFECTS. ALL KNOWLEDGE EXISTS as CAUSE. And it is simple. It is limited to LIGHT of MIND and the electric wave of motion which records God's thinking in matter."

Glenn Clark: "Can you tell me the process by which this ALL-KNOWLEDGE came to you? Was it always a gradual process, the result of earnest, patient seeking, or was there a high point, a period of revelation or illumination?"

Dr. Russell: "I will put it very simply, in May of 1921 God took me up into a high mountain of inspiration and intense ecstasy. A brilliant flash like lightning severed my bodily sensation from my consciousness and I found myself freed from my body and wholly in the Mind universe of Light, which is God…. And then God said to me, 'Behold thou the unity of all things in Light of Me, and the seeming separateness of all things in the two lights of my divided thinking. See thou that I, the Undivided, Unchanging One, am within all divided things, centering them, and I am without all changing things, controlling them.'"

Well, what does one say to that; we were just a couple of nineteen-year-old kids? Robert and I were so touched by *The Man Who Tapped the Secrets of the Universe*. We had never seen anything like that before. We proceeded to inquire. Who is this man? We were able to locate where the book was being sold, a place called The University of Science and Philosophy, Swannanoa, Waynesboro, Virginia. After further inquiry we received in the mail a brochure of the Russell writings. We ordered them all!

Another day I remember so well, the day Robert and I received a big box of Russell writings, not just by Walter Russell but writings penned by Lao Russell as well. Robert and I were flipping through the books. In one of the books, we came across a drawing. We were mesmerized. We just sat there staring at this drawing. What does it mean? Neither of us spoke. We just stared. For how long I don't remember. Did we know that this one picture from this one book would change the course of our lives forever? I would like to think that this one picture from this one book will change the world forever.

Walter and Lao Russell—*Atomic Suicide?*, 1957

This picture of *The Divine Trinity* became my philosophy if you will, perhaps more than just a philosophy but a spirituality. In short, the Russell's were presenting us with a with a new basis of the Universe/God. They present to us a sexual, i.e., procreative nature to the Universe. This was big! I came to realize that *The Divine Trinity* (that which I also call *The New Trintiy*) is the Metaphysical Given. It is primary/axiomatic (self-evident). We don't, nor can we, prove it. **But we must begin from it.** It presents to us the absolute of life/procreation—which, I might add, is our coherency. How many of the philosophers listed in this treatise touch life/procreation? And, if you will, make this distinction with me. *The United One is not the primary. Nor is the Divided Two the primary.* **The Primary of Life consists of <u>both</u> the Divided One and the United Two in balanced interchange together.** This is how I stated it in one of my writings.

...and the TWO shall become as ONE—Encoded in the Book of Eternal Life; Meditations for Deepening Love expanded edition © 2010

In the heart of every man and woman, the TWO, is placed the eternal desire to become as ONE. This desire is known as love. "May I give my life to you," the man shouts. "Yes, please do," the woman responds. And out of this love a new birth of life, a new born boy or girl, is brought forth as the eternal desire moves on. The ONE has just become the TWO again. This eternal process is called the *procreant*—a procreative process of balanced interchange between the TWO and the ONE.

And so the TWO becomes as ONE. Not a ONE of no TWO, but a TWO within a ONE for, procreantly, every ONE will again become a TWO. Within the ONE is always the divided TWO. Within the TWO is always the united ONE. And so the 'AS ONE' is actually a BALANCE between the dividing TWO and the uniting ONE. This balance is sexual in that the parts dividing and uniting are opposite pairs, opposite meaning sexual as in male and female pairs. *Sexual balanced interchange* is this procreant and eternal process, the ONE dividing into sexual opposites (the TWO) and the TWO uniting into the sexual equilibrium or rest of the ONE.

Let me continue with Robert's and my story. Along with the Russell books came a brochure of their writings. Included was information on their one-year home study course in Universal Law, Natural Science, and Living Philosophy. We proceeded to order that as well. We became immersed in the Russell material. In 1971, we heard from Lao Russell that she was having a get together of Russell students to celebrate the hundredth birthday of Walter Russell.* It was to be held at Swannanoa, Waynesboro, Virginia. Little did we know that Swannanoa was the home/palace of the literary, scientific, and artistic works of Walter Russell. Robert and I along with my brother Marc attended. When you first walk into the palace you think you have entered a new world. And Lao Russell gave us personal time. I remember her words well. She was talking to us about the fundamental message of the University of Science and Philosophy when she blurted out, *"And you have got to sex it you know."* Ok, and what does that mean? Does it mean that the universe is sexual in its nature? (How about God? Or philosophy itself?) Yes, that is what it means!

*Walter Russell passed in 1963.

On our return trip we were to fly out of Washington D.C. As we had a couple of hours waiting for our flight, we decided to go over to the Library of Congress. Lao Russell had mentioned a writing by Dr. Russell that was out of print. It was titled *The Universal One*, 1926. We inquired about it and was told it was out of print, or maybe it was that the copyright had expired. In any event, I asked the Library of Congress attendant if we could acquire a copy of it. Lo and behold, he said *"Yes."* A couple of weeks later I had a copy in my hands. I proceeded to make copies for Robert, my brother Marc, and a swimming buddy of mine, Mark Stanley. For the next ten plus years I studied the writings of Walter and Lao Russell. It was during this time that I returned to college in the study of philosophy. I was back home in California attending Sonoma State University. I wanted to know where Walter and Lao Russell fit, if at all, in the lineage of philosophy. Well, I don't know that they do. As I stated: "I came to realize that *The Divine Trinity* (that which I also call *The New Trintiy*) is the Metaphysical Given. It is primary and axiomatic (self-evident). We don't, nor can we, prove it. **But we must begin from it.** It presents to us the absolute of life/procreation—which, I might add, comprises our innate understanding/coherency of LIFE itself. How many of the philosophers listed in this treatise touch life/procreation?"

The following picture reveals what ought to be the basis of our philosophy and religion. The opposite two must be equal in necessity. *One is not without the other; both are needed for either to be.* Not secondary to some higher, unknowable, singular "God power" that we are called upon to worship. No, <u>primary</u>. Every life is PRIMARY to Life!

Let's take a moment and analyze the above picture. It equally includes **God the Mother**. Might we refer to Mother as Goddess? In any event, it encompasses both Father and Mother, i.e., Man and Woman. This Sexual Balance is also a Spiritual Balance. It is from this (Equal and Opposite) Balance that Procreation can and does occur. Please remember Procreation is not just physical; it is metaphysical/spiritual. Walter and Lao Russell never had children. Allow me to correct that statement. Their child was the University of Science and Philosophy which they created *together*. Each student of theirs was one of their *Spiritual Children*. I, myself, have never had a child. I have never been married. Always wanted a wife and children. So, what can I know? Well, I can know *Perfect Love*. You see, I found *Perfect Love* by first seeing it—in you!

To Cassandra—Early Years © 1985, 1994

A Miracle For You

Deep within each heart
There lies a light
That shines with love
For another to see.
But this light
Lies so deep within
That only a few
Have ever seen it shine.
Yet, every now and then
For some unknown reason
One's light
Begins to shine through.
And for a reason still unknown
Suddenly, there is a light
At this very instant
Shining through
Behold! It is your light
And now another can see.

When I was in my late twenties, having spent the last ten or so years studying the Russell writings, I had an experience I will never forget. Suddenly, seemingly out of nowhere, a flash of light entered my head. I heard the words, **"Your purpose is to bring the Message of Man and Woman Balance to planet earth!"** Well, maybe that explains why I have never been married or had children.* The **purpose** was overwhelming and all consuming. It was from this experience that I began to write myself—slowly forming the conception of a **New Trinity**. This was the purpose presented to me. It first had to be completed. I had no idea of the time and rigor it would require. I was already turning my attention more towards New Thought (Thomas Troward, Neville Goddard), Eastern Thought (Sri Ramakrishna), Christian Mysticism (Meister Eckhart, Martin Buber, Leo Tolstoy) Sexual Metaphysics (Sigmund Freud, Wilhelm Reich, D. H. Lawrence) as well as *A Course in Miracles*. Instead of Socrates, Plato, and Aristotle, I was into Emerson, Thoreau, and Whitman. Speaking of Whitman, let's complete this section with these quotes from his writing *Leaves of Grass*.

*May a woman come forth to receive/reproduce this message.

Walt Whitman (1819-1892)—*Leaves of Grass: Song for Myself* (First Edition) 1855

"I have heard what the talkers were talking…
the talk of the beginning and the end,
But I do not talk of the beginning or the end.
There was never any more inception than there is now,
Nor any more youth or age than there is now;
And will never be any more perfection than there is now,
Nor any more heaven or hell than there is now.
Urge and urge and urge,
Always the procreant urge of the world.
Out of the dimness opposite equals advance…Always substance and increase.
Always a knit of identity….always distinction….always a breed of life."

Walt Whitman (1819-1892)—*Leaves of Grass: Sing the Body Electric* (First Edition) 1855

"This is the nucleus…after the child is born of woman the man is born of woman,
This is the bath of birth…this is the merge of small and large and the outlet again."

Did Walt Whitman make the procreant distinction as well? Sounds like it! Thank you, Walt Whitman.

A Life Given

"Enough!"

Stanley Maynard Anderson
May 21, 1919 - August 9, 1998

Preface

Might we ever understand that the sole purpose of (corrupt) government is to take control of our pocketbooks? We, in America, thought we were free. Afterall, didn't we fight a war of independence? It appears we are still fighting for it. *A Life Given* is the true story about my Father and myself; what we went through during the years of 1992-1998. Before we begin, I would like to list some quotes from some renown authors.

Henry David Thoreau (1817-1862)— American author and poet
"There will never be a really free and enlightened State until the State comes to recognize the individual as a higher and independent power, from which all its own power and authority are derived, and treats him accordingly."

Ayn Rand (1905-1982)—author and philosopher
"The right to life is the source of all rights—and the right to property is their only implementation. Without property rights, no other rights are possible."

"The [U.S.] Constitution is a limitation on the government, not on private individuals ... it does not prescribe the conduct of private individuals, only the conduct of the government ... it is not a charter for government power, but a charter of the citizen's protection against the government."

"Money is the barometer of a society's virtue. When you see that trading is done, not by consent, but by compulsion—when you see that in order to produce, you need to obtain permission from men who produce nothing—when you see that money is flowing to those who deal, not in goods, but in favors—when you see that men get richer by graft and by pull than by work, and your laws don't protect you against them, but protect them against you—when you see corruption being rewarded and honesty becoming a self-sacrifice—you know that your society is doomed."

Thomas Paine (1737-1809)—American political writer
"Money, when considered as the fruit of many years' industry, as the reward of labor, sweat and toil, is not to be supported with, or trusted to the airy bubble of paper currency."

Fredrich August von Hayek (1899-1992)—economist
"The history of government management of money has, except for a few short happy periods, been one of incessant fraud and deception."

Thomas Jefferson (1743-1826)—3rd President of the United States
"I sincerely believe…that banking establishments are more dangerous than standing armies, and that the principle of spending money to be paid by posterity under the name of funding is but swindling futurity on a large scale.

"Were we directed from Washington when to sow, and when to reap, we should soon want bread."

Ezra Pound (1885-1972)—American poet
"Wars in old times were made to get slaves. The modern implement of imposing slavery is debt."

And let's not forget this quote. One of the great quotes from one of our Founding Fathers.

James Madison (1751-1836)—Founding Father and 4th United States President
"As a man is said to have a right to his property, he may be equally said to have a property in his rights. Where an excess of power prevails, property of no sort is duly respected. No man is safe in his opinions, his person, his faculties, or his possessions."

Now, you might be asking, why are we including *A Life Given* in a treatise on **Spiritual Procreation/Eternal Life**. It is because the idea of balance (Rhythmic Balanced Interchange/Equal and Opposite) runs through all things from the microscopic to the macroscopic. And it certainly includes economic balance, i.e. **Sovereignty, Freedom, Unalienable Rights, and Liberty and Justice for all**. We, the people, are not somebody else's corporation/servant but are **Sovereign Living Procreant Beings**. But how can we get to a balance with another if we do not have a balanced metaphysics within ourselves going in?

Introduction

"Bye-bye-ya. Thank you. Thank you. Bye-bye-ya." Those were the last words my father spoke to me just days before his passing. In his death, my father gave of his life. In his giving, his spirit was perfected and he found an eternal life. I say this because my father had two things happen to him shortly before his death that I believe to be miraculous. I want to tell you about these two things because, I believe, they give meaning to the idea of spiritual perfection. To do so, I must begin with some background on my father so you can better understand his experience. I will complete this section with these miraculous events. I am sharing about my father simply because I don't want his spirit and what he stood for to ever be forgotten.

My father was born on May 21, 1919 in Parlier, California. He was the youngest of seven children. His parents were immigrants from Sweden who had settled and farmed in the Central Valley. When he was ten years old, his mother died. Three years later his father passed away leaving him, along with his sister, with much of the responsibility of running the farm. After high school, he attended Reedley Junior College and then the University of California at Berkeley where his ambition was to study law. With the uneasiness of war approaching, he began taking flying lessons—he didn't want to be in the "walking Army," as he would later say. In 1941, he made the decision to apply to United Air Lines and was accepted into United's first aviation school. He was the youngest member of that first class of graduates. He began his flying career in the DC-3 and ended it in 1979 as the number one (senior) captain flying the 747 on the San Francisco-Hawaii run. It was on one of my father's early flights that he met my mother, Mary Jane Norvill, who was then a stewardess. They were soon married, eventually settling in the San Francisco Bay Area. I am the youngest of four sons.

In 1961, my father, along with a partner, bought the historical eight-hundred acre Wikiup Rancho in Santa Rosa. It is hard to believe, but for close to twenty years my father worked two full-time and demanding jobs, one as an airline captain and the other as a land developer and sometimes builder. You might think that as a child growing up, I saw little of him. Actually, that was not the case. He seemed to always make time for us and I remember our family doing many things together. My father really believed in family. He had so much love in his heart for us. That is what I remember most about him, his incredible love. He would read to us the poetry, philosophy, and Biblical scriptures he loved so much. He could quote from memory just about anything he had read. He was always striving to better himself and take on some new project. Often, he would speak about the greater person that lay within each of us. My father really was what you would call a self-made man.

One of my father's greatest convictions was that of productive work. He strove to accomplish his goals. He really believed that if one was left to one's own initiative that one could accomplish most anything. That is why he took on the Wikiup project. He had never done anything that big before but he didn't appear to have much or any fear about it. It was his vision. He and his partner had the project master-planned, acquired the necessary county permits and approvals, and went to work. For the first few years everything seemed to be going well. Then something happened. My father and his partner ran into a wall called governmental politics. The approved master plan had called for sewer installation which was necessary for the majority of the development. Suddenly, for no apparent reason, sewer expansion was denied and the project was stalled. It wasn't too long after that that my father's partner wanted out so my father now had the whole financial burden placed upon himself. For years the land just stood there—with mortgages and taxes to pay. My father tried everything to get sewer to the property, even spending hundreds of thousands of dollars on studies to have it built on Wikiup property. And the land just sat there.

During this time of frustration for my father, I was still fairly young—junior high and high school. I didn't really understand my father's burden and his growing anguish. He was being blocked from his vision and work—to support his family—and didn't understand why. Sometimes I would hear him mutter to himself *"pigs at the pub-*

lic trough," in reference to county officials and government in general. Something was wrong, but what? That was the question.

In the late sixties, I went off to college—I suppose to "find" myself. That really didn't work out and after a couple of years, I returned to Santa Rosa. Through the seventies I worked part time for my father and took philosophy courses at the local university. It was during these years that I was developing the ideas that would later comprise the philosophy of what I call *Man and Woman Balance*. At the time, it was my brother, Marc, who was working directly with my father on the Wikiup and sewer problem. Marc's work in getting the sewer included in the area's new specific plan was most crucial.

In 1980, I came to work for my father full-time.* He was now retired from the airline and was devoting himself to the Wikiup development. Marc was getting married and was ready to move on. I took over his job. My first task was to get the sewer project through. It took four years but we got sewer. My father was so pleased—it had taken some sixteen years. He was finally able to pay off most of the mortgages and breathe. We still had lots of work to do and my father was not one to sit still. For the next eight years he and I worked side-by-side on the Wikiup and other ventures. Without even knowing it, we were growing very close. We would spend countless hours together talking about spiritual matters, philosophy, social-political issues, economics, etc. We just enjoyed each other's company. By now I understood what my father had been through and I, too, felt something was wrong. My father had lost hundreds of thousands, if not millions, of dollars in governmental delays but our sense was that the problem was much bigger than just Wikiup.

*One of the perks of working for my father was that it also gave me a chance to write. Over the next fourteen years, I wrote many of the books on Man and Woman Balance.

By 1991, most of Wikiup was completed. We also had completed a project in Hawaii. All and all, things were looking pretty good. We built a house on the last remaining property in Wikiup and moved our operations there. My father and I had been working this property for many years, growing a vegetable garden and small orchard of fruit trees, and we both loved it. For me, it was not an easy decision to move in with my parents. I was still single and wanted a family of my own. My father was having some health problems and, I think, I knew in my heart that I would need to be there for him. I just believed it all would work out somehow, and that when I did meet the right woman that she would understand. Anyway, my Dad was in the new house on the property he loved. He finally felt he could slow down. He began to read more. Of course, we continued our evening talks. But before he could really relax, something happened that was to forever change our lives. We both would come to understand just what was wrong.

It was in 1992 that we received word from our accountant that the IRS wanted to audit us. (I guess that is what happens when one finally makes a little money!) The audit started with one of our corporations, moved to the other one, and finally ended with my parents themselves. The audit itself lasted nearly two years. By the time it was over the IRS was demanding close to $450,000. (That did not include the $150,000. or so the state would want.) We didn't have those kinds of liquid assets (cash) and would have had to liquidate our few remaining properties. Here was my father, having worked two jobs most of his life, even having served his country transporting supplies via United Air Lines in time of war, having raised a family, now at the twilight of his life, and someone says to him (at virtual gunpoint), "Give us your money." The IRS was essentially saying to him, "Your life was in vain." What was he supposed to do, start over? And then what? You know, it really makes one wonder—*who are these people?*

Have you ever experienced raw terror? That is what my father and I felt. Hopelessness, despair, a black hole sucking our insides out; that is what it is like to face the undefined monster called the IRS. My own life was at risk, too. Besides being president of the corporations, I had my writings to consider. My own progression and success with these writings was tied into my success at Wikiup. But the thing that disturbed me the most was the IRS essentially telling my father—*"Your life does not matter."** My father was a great man; **his life did matter**. His life mattered even if he hadn't worked two jobs, supported his country, or raised a family. **My Dad mattered**. And so did my Mom who lived through every moment of this. If he, and also she, did not matter then who does? Do you understand this? **You matter, too.** Everyone matters. It's called *spiritual sovereigncy*.

*During this time my Father had gone to the Church he and my Mom attended. They were co-founders of it! He just wanted some solace, some encouragement and support. None was forth coming. In fact, he was told that he, my father, must be in the wrong. I guess to the Church Elders his life did not matter. Broke his heart.

That evening after my father and I had received the results of the audit, we were sitting in his office. There was a deathly silence about us. You could feel the darkness, almost evil. Suddenly, seemingly out of nowhere, my father turned to me, looked me right in the eye, and calmly but firmly uttered one word. ENOUGH! Can you imagine the force of mind, the strength of character, the courage that comes from the willingness to put everything on the line to utter that one word? **ENOUGH!** One word—it pierced my heart; my world was never to be the same again. Please understand, we had no idea of what to do; we knew as little about the IRS as everyone else. Nevertheless, the next day we parted company with our CPA and started out on our own. We started from *nothing*—to take on what may be the biggest criminal organization our world has ever known. We had to learn everything from scratch. I mean, how do you even go about finding out who these people are and just where they get their authority? We had to develop a strategy for our economic survival. I won't go into detail here about what we did. Let's just say we struggled day and night for four years. I call it our four years of hell. My father had handed me the ball. Just as I had to bring sewer to Wikiup, now I had to get rid of the "sewer" (IRS) out of Wikiup. Same battle, against the same mysterious foe, just different in size. My father never wavered in his faith in me or our cause. (He would often remind me of the Biblical verse Hebrews 11:1: *Now faith is the substance of things hoped for, and the evidence of things not seen.*) Every strategy I developed, every letter I wrote and sent out, every strain I felt, he was aware of. He pushed hard. And, of course, I could not let him down. He was my father.

Sometimes it takes great adversity to push through to a clearer vision. Our experience with the IRS certainly was that adversity. But through this experience we came to understand just what was wrong, from my father's struggles with Wikiup to our IRS problems. In short, what was and still is wrong is that we are no longer free. The freedom we thought we had no longer existed or perhaps never existed. We the people certainly lost our freedom through the bankruptcy of the United States government in 1933* where we, the sovereign people, were made the debtor slaves of the banker creditors. It is this invisible hand of the money changers, i.e., banking cartel that keeps us in debt/bondage through their phony money scheme. This invisible hand has been working hundreds, if not thousands, of years to perfect its counterfeit money scheme. Who are these people? I could go on and on about this but let me just quote from the German poet Goethe (1749–1832): *"None are more hopelessly enslaved than those who falsely believe they are free."* Or the James Madison quote from earlier, *"…Where an excess of power prevails, property of no sort is duly respected…."*

*Perhaps we lost our freedoms in 1871 when, after the Civil War, we became a corporate extension of the City of London. Perhaps we never really got free of Great Britain in the American Revolution.

By 1996, we were almost free from the IRS. They had succeeded in placing a lien on my parents. (It is actually called a *Notice of Federal Tax Lien Under IRS Laws*. What does that tell you?) Once one of these liens is recorded in the County Recorder's Office, it takes on a life of its own. My investigation of this lien led me to Section 2102 of the Uniform Federal Lien Registration Act—which is California state law—which states that a lien must be certified (properly signed and notarized) before recordation. How convenient that the IRS skips this step and that the County Recorders look the other way. Thousands of IRS liens are filed daily across this country, and, I suspect, not one of them is properly (legally) certified in violation of states' laws. I, with the help of a legal scholar friend, brought this "miscue" to the attention of the County Recorder. I wanted the lien "unrecorded" for lack of certification. The County Recorded refused.

A few months prior to this, I had attended a sovereignty workshop in San Francisco. After the County Recorder's refusal, I called the sponsor of the workshop for any ideas about the lien. Through a series of calls, I was led to a man that was to play an important role in my father's spiritual perfection. His name is Ronald Peter MacDonald. Ron has been gifted with a spiritual understanding of the law. He is not an attorney but a legal scholar. When I first met Ron, I explained to him our situation and asked him if he could help. He said, *"Yes!"* Within a few months, and with Ron's help, I filed a suit in State Court against the County Recorder for allowing the IRS to record a lien without proper certification. The case ended up in Federal Court in San Francisco and was heard in February of 1997. The Attorney for the United Stated Department of Justice sought to have the case thrown out claiming the United States (or IRS) had immunity from suit from anyone (any "debtor" actually) bringing a case against the United States who had a "beneficial interest." The Attorney for the County of Sonoma also sought the case's dismissal claiming I could not represent my parents even if I did have power of attorney from them. Ron foresaw these attacks and had structured the paperwork so that it was actually a case of public interest in having the laws of the State of California adhered to. This was the basis of my oral arguments. I appeared twice in federal court and by the second appearance the United States Attorney and the Attorney for the County of Sonoma had lost their arguments. In fact, Ron's strategy so unnerved the judge that she abruptly stopped the proceedings and walked out of the courtroom. She didn't recuse herself but later issued a ruling to derail this case and broke federal statute to do so. I won't get into all the technicalities here—clearly this case represented a threat to the powers that be and their debt/bondage scheme. Ron and I decided not to pursue the case for personal reasons but we now knew what it would take to return the power back to the people. There will be another day.

Even though we were not able to prevail in federal court on the IRS lien, my father was very proud of our efforts. He had read all of Ron's paperwork and understood the concept of the public interest as the opening to reclaim our sovereignty. He knew we would all have to stand up one day and say to the money changers— ENOUGH—just as he had said. The lien on my parents was not doing any real damage because, at this time, they didn't have any property in their own name. Nevertheless, my father, and myself as well, could feel its debt/bondage in our souls. This issue was brought to a head towards the end of 1997 when I uncovered through a Preliminary Title Report that a property my parents had previously owned was being clouded by this IRS lien. Needless-to-say, this could have resulted in legal ramifications against my parents. This greatly worried my father as he wanted everything to be cleaned up. He wanted to be free. I asked Ron to look into this matter. The first indications were that the Title Company would not remove mention of the lien from the Title Report.

In early February, 1998, my father had a seizure. I heard my mother scream and I ran upstairs. Seeing my father unconsciousness, I instructed my mother to call 911 and held my father in my arms (so he could breathe and not choke on his blood) as we waited for the ambulance. I whispered to him, *"I'm here, Papa, I got you. I won't let you go. It is not your time yet."* My father was hospitalized for eight days but he did pull through. My mother and I visited him three times every day, just to be with him. When we got him home, we nursed him. He was very weak but slowly began to regain his strength. Towards the end of April, my father began to experience difficulty in reading and writing. He would skip or misspell or misread words. We initially thought this was due to the heavy anti-seizure medication he was taking. We didn't realize at the time that his passing had already been determined.

By the middle of May, Ron had completed his research on the lien and the Title Report. A letter was sent to the Title Company. In less than forty-eight hours, the Title Company issued a new Title Report minus any mention of the IRS lien. When I got word of this, I ran up to my Father's room and said, "Dad, I have something to tell you. (He could still hear and speak.) "What is it?" he asked. "Clear Title!" My father was overjoyed. ***"It's a miracle,"*** he said. It was for, in that moment, he knew that he was now (spiritually) free and that the IRS could not touch him, nor my mother or me. My father now knew that the spiritual decision he made within himself when he uttered the word **ENOUGH** some four plus years earlier was the right decision and no, his life had not been in vain.

Inwardly, my father was free of the nation-state and now he could rest.

Because of my father's worsening condition, we took him to a specialist. The news was not good. My father had a brain tumor. He would not consider radiation or surgery, both long shots at best. I think we all knew in our hearts that this was going to be his final call. But he was ready. He was free. His heart was at peace. His spirit was perfected. For now, let me just say that my father walked into his death without fear. His only wish was to die at home with his loved ones. In those last months, my mother and I took care of him. He never complained about anything. Well, every once in awhile he would look into my eyes and say, *"I want to go home."* Although he was slowly losing consciousness, his spirit (love) only seemed to grow. Family and friends who visited him during these last months were so moved by his love and joy. A couple of weeks before his passing, I was sitting on his bed next to him saying, *"Papa, your spirit is perfected; you have gone full circle."* He could barely whisper at this time and I wasn't even sure he understood me. After a moment had passed, my father gently lifted up his hand and drew a circle in the air with his finger. We just looked at each other for an *eternal* moment. He knew. In the last days, we would lay together for hours on end. He would lay his head on my belly and I would gently stroke his head. Why? Why do all these things? I wanted to make sure his spirit stayed fully open all the way to the end. One little imbalance at this most sensitive time could cause it to constrict.

One morning when my mother and I were attending to my father, she looked up at me and cried out, *"I can't go on anymore."* She was exhausted. Neither one of us was getting much sleep. I said to her, *"If God has given us the task of allowing Dad to go in this way, he certainly has given us the energy to do so."* Within a few minutes my mother had her strength back. (This event was to change her spirit.) The next day she and my father were lying on the bed together, their heads at the foot of the bed, uttering their last words of love to each other. The day after my father slipped into unconsciousness and died two days later. The morning of my father's passing, I felt his spirit leave his body. I said to my mother,

"Dad's spirit has now left him." It was a spirit that had been perfected.

I am including some letters in this section that my father had written to me and to the family in general over the years. He was a prolific letter writer and had written a family letter for years. These letters are from after the time I began to work with him. Also included are a few of my letters to him, as well as some letters from friends during his last days. It is my sincere hope that you, the reader, will be able to see the depth of my father's love, not just for my sake, but in respect to the *life stand* he made. It is my sincere hope that my father will never be forgotten.

Letters

Dear Dad,   May 21, 1982

Just wanted to tell you how nice it is to be working with you. I know we don't work together all that often but I am learning a great deal; more importantly, I am coming to understand the effort you have put in over the years and I deeply appreciate you, not just because you are my father but because I really believe in you and your dream, and your right to freely pursue it.

I have always thought you were a fine man. You have an inner glow, joy, and optimism that just makes everyone feel good. I think you are by nature a very kind and gentle person. I know it must be very difficult to always "tow the line."

I feel I in my own life have come to support you in whatever you need to carry on. I do hope you will be able to take some time in the near future to relax and reflect on the stirrings in your mind.

I want you to know that I feel very close to you and love you very much.

Happy Birthday,

Love Chris

To Family:*   July, 4, 1984

I am writing to you on Independence Day to see if you feel independent. In America we say that independence (our Declaration of Independence) means freedom. Initially, it was freedom from the bonds of the King of England. Actually, from the whole feudal system of Europe.

*My father wrote many family letters like this that went to many of his relatives.

This is 1984. And this is the year that Orwell said that big government would take away our freedom. Big Brother would be looking over our shoulders all of the time.

I reveled in the year 1976. That was the Bicentennial of United States freedom; our two-hundredth year freedom anniversary.

Are we really aware that during most of man's history he lived under despotism? There were the Pharaohs; and then the Judges: and the Kings, and the Caesars, and the Czars, and then the Dictators. All of whom had power over life and death with the snap of a finger on a whim. There was nothing you or your family or your friends could do about it. There has only been about two hundred years of light in man's history, most of which we have had here in these United States.

During your and my lifetime, we have lived under the greatest freedom in the history of the world,* in the richest nation the world has ever seen. A time in history when men who proceeded us carved out a proclamation that declared we are endowed with certain Inalienable Rights, among which are Life, Liberty, and the Pursuit of Happiness. This document has made the United States the greatest state that ever was.

* My father was later to have a change of mind.

During our lifetime we have enjoyed this greatest freedom, this greatest material wealth, the greatest multiplication of knowledge, the best opportunity for enlightenment and understanding. These should have brought us the best personal contentment in the history of mankind. So let us be very happy with our blessings.

Cordially,

Stan

To Dad   June, 1986

What is a Father?

A father is one

Who will take the place

Of his son

Most willingly

When his son is feeling pain

Yet knows

This he cannot do

If his son is to grow up

And someday

Become a father too.

Dear Son, December 23, 1986

Mom and I were in the ocean at 9:15 this morning and watched your flight take-off. We wished you "Bon Voyage" from the sea! And then, neither one of us said very much and by the time we returned to the apartment we missed you so much independently, that we finally broke the news to each other that we were sad because our son was not here anymore. We had such a wonderful week here in Hawaii with you; it was so fun being with you and swimming with you, and visiting with you. And last night especially, talking with you in the pool, hearing of your ideas, goals, and directives, like a laser, beaming out in the direction that you want to go.

You are a serious fellow, trying to comprehend, trying to understand, and trying to solve the problem of the "abyss." I, too, was greatly fearful and greatly concerned about these things in my youth. But when I took up the Scriptures at age thirty, I received great comfort. The Prophets and Apostles and Disciples wrote that some things are not given for us to know, but that one day we shall come into this knowledge. I keep my mind occupied these days by being thankful for everything I have; first of all, my wonderful wife and sons, and then each beautiful day, and for each little blessing that comes.

But this day we can't help but feel sad because we love you so much, and miss you. On the other hand, we rejoice because you have not gone for long. Only taken a flight away. I guess I took several thousand of those over the years away from you. But we are looking forward to joining you again at Wikiup to again visit and discourse in fellowship. In the meantime, "Bon Voyage," our son. We trust for a nice flight and hope that when you get home you miss us a little, too, and call us with news of your safe arrival.

Love,

Dad, and Mom too!

Dad,   1989

   Just a few thoughts that came to me in the night:

   -All we have is each other.

   -Let us strive to be accountable for our thoughts.

   -Let's acknowledge our temptations, consciously in our minds, yet know that they do not have our spirits.

Chris

Merry Christmas to Chris,   December 25, 1989

   You are indeed a Jewel of a Son. And we appreciate you and love you more than the spoken word can tell.

All of our love,

Dad and Mom

Dad,   June, 1991

Thoughts to consider:*

-Do not blame, complain, or criticize. It can only make the situation worse.

-Ask for what you want; do not demand to receive it.

-We each are responsible for our own internal experience.

-Everything we do we, on some level, choose to do.

-The other person's life is as important to him or her as our own life is to ourselves.

-Reality is a relationship, created out of the interaction of two or more people.

-All we have is this moment that we are creating together now.

Chris

*My Dad responded: "This was helpful to me and I set up a personal policy—Don't complain! Don't Blame! Don't Explain!

To Family,   July, 1993

Hawaii

 We were walking along the beach and looked out at the water. I said, "Oh thou great, blue, beautiful ocean; roll on, roll!" And do you know what? A wave lifted itself off of the surface, rolled right to me, and spread itself out at my feet! Now that is power! I don't mean mine. I mean of the ocean.

 We feel like a part of nature over here. Dressed in the skimpiest attire to blend in with the temperature, swaying along with the palms, rolling with the ocean. As a matter of fact, we are all more than that; we are all children of the universe, no less than the trees and the stars. We have a right to be here. And, whether or not it is clear to us, no doubt the universe is unfolding as it should. Remember, with all of its sham, drudgery, and unfulfilled dreams; it still can be a beautiful world. The choice is ours. *"The Kingdom of God is within us."* Luke 17:21*

Aloha Kakahiaka!

Beach Bum,

Stan

*This and the next letter are examples of my father's philosophy of life.

To Family,   October, 1993

    The supreme mystery of the great wide universe is life. We come here without our consent; from whence, we know not. We depart without our consent; whither, we know not.

    Through the centuries our best thinkers have tried to solve this riddle. Why? Because we want to know. That we are placed on this earth for a reason and purpose is not doubted by most serious thinkers. Is it not possible that the power that placed us here has a plan for us even after we depart?

    May it not be advisable for us to cooperate by assuming responsibility for control of our conduct while here, to the end that we may be decent to one another and do all the good we can in all the ways we can during this life?

    Is it not also possible for us to accept the why? And the desire to know through faith; which is the only channel discovered to date?

    "The happiest hearts that daily beat are in those quiet breasts that find the common daylight sweet and leave to heaven the rest."*

Cordially,

Stan

*I believe my father was quoting someone else—perhaps it was John Vance Cheney (1848-1922).

Dear Chris,   October 1, 1993

I believe we both recently have walked through the Valley of Baca (Tears)*, but let it now become a place of springs where pools of blessing and refreshment collect after rains.

Let us be bathed and climb out of the valley onto the mountain tops where we rise above these current problems; IRS and slow sales and leasing, and from where we can see our best course.

Will you believe with me that we can form a Master Mind group, which includes Jesus ("*Where two or more are gathered together in my name, there am I in the midst of them.*" Matthew 18:20) to respond to and see us through this IRS and also to include our sales and leasing problems? Please answer this question.

"*And all things whatsoever ye ask in prayer, believing, ye shall receive.*" Matthew 24:35

Love Dad

P.S. Thank you for helping arrange a work space which includes me.

* My father wrote me this letter some days after he had said that one word ENOUGH regarding the IRS.

To Family,   March, 1994

It's Tax Season

The First Thief

The government is the first thief.* IRS employees know this, and they become the second thief. Crooks see this and become the third thief, by example.

This whole system of ever-increasing taxation and regulation to maintain the vested interests of a huge bureaucracy will crumble as did the communist system.

Bureaucracy by any other name is still bureaucracy. It matters not if you label it communism, fascism, or democracy.

The users need to be producers by doing something useful.

As soon as the people understand what is going on, they will change it. Tell your neighbor!

Cordially,

Stan

*This and the next few letters reveal my father's thoughts on what has been happening to our country.

To Family,   May, 1994

Another war for freedom's sustenance has commenced. How many times since our founding Fathers envisioned a free America has her sons fought to sustain it? I well remember W.W. II and my various escapades in it. Always in the air, thank the Lord.

And then there was Korea. Then Vietnam. My, how worrying was that war, now that I had sons old enough to be called up. Son Marc, an Air Force Reservist, was called but they sent him to England. Mother and I and his brother, Chris, flew over to see how the war was going there. Marc was stationed at Mindenhall Air Force Base, which was near a girls' college. Marc got he and Chris dates, who took them out on the Moors to see the Downs of Heather. Or was it down in the heather to see the Moors? My, how those English know how to handle a war. They usually call upon the Americans to save the world from whatever.

Then my son Chris went into the Air Force. They sent him to Texas. I was the only one who went to Vietnam. Yah, the old man; by then fifty-five but still in the air, thank the Lord. So here I am, seventy-five this month, and my doctors say, dying. But what do they know?

There's nothing like a war to wake you up. This war is different from any we have had before. Yet, it is for freedom again, but the enemy has invaded and already taken over. They are aliens and work surreptitiously with guile and trickery. The American people complacently going about trying to earn a living don't seem to know what is happening. Posing as regular people, just working for government, these aliens are bent on replacing the Constitution with their own regulations, making the American people their slaves. Only a few of us old-timers steeped in the history of the struggle for liberty seem to know what is going on.

Americans Awaken!

This is a call to battle. And when the battle's done Liberty shall be won, again.

Cordially,

Stan

Good-by Gestapo—Hello Freedom*

A class action lawsuit was filed against the Internal Revenue Service, Commissioner of the IRS, District Directors and all other delegated agents by 450 litigants in the U.S. District Court, Central Division, Utah on April 21, 1994. This group of freedom-loving Americans from all over the country learned of this contemplated action by word of mouth and joined. Work to date has necessarily proceeded without publicity, but now as press releases are made, other litigants are welcome. There is a window of opportunity of approximately 90 days for anyone to add his or her name as a participant.

*This letter was printed in the Retired United Pilots Association (RUPA) Newsletter from which one retired pilot, Dave Fuller, called my Dad. Dave helped us in our battle with the IRS. This class action lawsuit was part of the wave of discontent that led to the IRS hearings in Congress in 1998 that essentially did nothing to correct the money scam.

It seems to me that millions of Americans sense something is wrong in our country but haven't quite known what it is. I believe our economic life-blood is being sucked away by bureaucrats through mismanagement, waste, and criminal fraud. Bureaucrat is another name for government employee. This starts at the top and, by example, filters down through all levels in departments of the three branches of government. It took the confirmation of the GAO findings in their IRS audit to arouse enough good citizens to the livid level of action.

Not only are individuals aroused concerning the continuing violation of the Constitution by government employees, but so are various states, as evidenced in the resolution passed today by the State of Colorado legislature: "serving Notice and Demand to the federal government to cease and desist; effective immediately; mandates that are beyond the scope of its constitutionally delegated powers."

The attorneys for the plaintiffs are experienced and capable in litigation in the field of Constitutional law, taxation, and civil rights and have successfully represented claimants in other litigation of this nature. There are eight counts in this court action, the first of which demands that the GAO audit be completed and the results published and made available for scrutiny by the general public. The audit was dropped when the IRS stated they couldn't produce actual records and did not keep inventories of equipment or repossessed property. (When I learned there was only a one-year audit and the IRS had eighty years of the same, I turned livid.)

We are dealing with a three-pronged approach:

In the Courts—Seeking declaratory relief and judgments from fraud, deception, and illegal practices of IRS employees.

Politically—already over a dozen congressmen have called for details on our action plan and an alternative to the IRS. They are now standing in line to sponsor a bill and become heroes. That's O.K. No one in this complaint cares who gets the credit. We just don't want our children to have to crouch down and lick the hands of those setting chains upon them.

Strength of the people—Liberty lies in the hearts of people, but if it dies there, no court can help it. We need people, thousands and thousands of people. An enemy within is more difficult than an enemy without. The enemy, our government, is already within, but if people now will rally, we will win.

There is a well-formulated Freedom Tax replacement for the 123,000 IRS coterie; which provides for no federal deduction from paychecks, no tax on saving, pension, retirement, medical services, food, items of clothing over $50., or personal residences.

Stan

Retired United Pilots:

Headline:* During the 15 years since my retirement, I have read the RUPA News each month and recall only one contributor who has indicated he knew anything about the planned New World Order that President Bush announced in 1989.

*This letter was also printed in the RUPA news. You might think my father was becoming an advocate of the conspiracy theory of history. Well, ask yourself—"Do you have clear title to your own property or money—or life?"

Subsequent to my letters offering booklets and bibliographies on this subject, I have received a multitude of requests, with the writer often also relating an account of his harassment, intimidation, and coercion by the IRS. My reply has been, "And you thought your country (the land of the free and home of the brave) wouldn't wreck this havoc on you. It didn't!

Eustice Mullins who spent 38 years researching and writing about the Federal Reserve and IRS syndicates says, "The Federal Reserve System is not federal; it has no reserves; and is not a system but rather a private criminal syndicate, the product of an international consortium. The IRS is its private collection agency which originated as the Blanc Hand in medieval Italy as collectors of debt by force and extortion for the ruling Italian mob families." Neither of these syndicates are part of the U.S. government, but pose as such. They were initially set up by agents and collaborators on the European Rothchild and Warburg syndicates.

In 1776 in Germany, Adam Weishaupt and Mayer Amschel Rothchild founded the Illuminati, a secret organization with a vision and a master plan to control the whole world under an "illuminated leadership." Today, secret societies in the U.S. variously known as the Insiders, the International Bankers, Illuminati, Bilderbergers, Council of Foreign Relations, Tri-lateral Commission, etc., are all parts in the assembly of the United Nations New World Order, which is better called the Conspiracy. I can relate the whole history to you from its inception, but not in one letter.

The conspiracy, though its multitude of syndicates and agents, has immense economic and political influence. Through its control of our nation's banks, media, and politicians it has controlled the

Congress and all agencies of the executive branch for the past fifty years. Clinton is only a puppet, as were Bush, Reagan, Carter, Nixon, and even Eisenhower. The whole scheme is based on a passion for money and power, primarily employing secrecy, deceit, and cunning, but stopping at nothing; murders, engineered wars, depression, money panics; whatever it takes. Without conscience, morality, or mercy; "the end justifies the means." Some of the translators working from the original investigative reports were so shocked they could only work one hour per day. So have been I! We wrestle not only against flesh and blood, but also against principalities and powers in high places, which is best called the New Babylon.

This letter is an attempt to "awaken the town and tell the people." Whether or not it is clear to you, my courageous colleagues, you are going to have to fight if you want your children and grandchildren to have any semblance of the life you have had. Freedom does not come for free. It must be defended continuously. So prepare yourselves unto the battle. I am not suggesting you fight in a posse comitatus under your County Shire-reev, but that you fight with the courageous and compassionate principal of noblesse oblige. Education is our strategy, and truth is our weapon. How can those led by the "father of lies" with only lies, deceit, and all that is evil, for tools, prevail?

Here is the good news. The war has already been won! We are only participating in the remaining battles. The war was won 1994 years ago by the love of God at Calvary. As for the future, John tells us in the Apocalypse: *"Babylon the Great is fallen, is fallen...All nations have drunk of the wine of her...and the merchants of the earth are waxed rich through the abundance of her delicacies...and the kings of the earth who have committed fornication and lived deliciously with her, shall bewail her, and lament her, when they shall see the smoke of her burning... And every shipmaster, and all the company in ships, and sailors, and as many as trade by sea stood afar...for the fear of her torment, and cried when they saw the smoke of her burning."* Revelation 18

Indeed, God is allowing us to live in interesting times. And what is His message to Christians? *"Come out of her my people. That you be not partakers of her sins, and that you receive not of her plagues."* Revelation 18:4

Stan Anderson

Chris, August 31, 1994

Mom and I really appreciate all of the things you do around here. How you have taken responsibility for all of the irrigating, all of the gardening, and now all of the IRS problem. You have made yourself indispensable. God bless you on your birthday.

With love,

Dad and Mom

Dear Family, July 28, 1995

Enclosed is a package that Chris has created and served by certified mail to all those named and/or shown on the c.c. list. I am so proud of Chris that I could burst. He has taken hold of this private Mafia criminal syndicate called the IRS and is shaking their legs like a bulldog would shake a robber intruder into his territory. Chris works all day researching and writing on the word processor, and then stays awake half the night mentally reviewing his work and making corrections, etc. He has set aside his own dreams and ambitions to help on this job, and is not able these days to get his own work done. I think he is making this sacrifice to help his father. I carried this yoke of oppression the last couple of years, but Chris is doing a much better job in this phase than I could have ever done. He has brought to the battle the armament of reasonableness, using correct law alone as his tools, carefully quoting current legal statutes by title, section, and paragraph, i.e., United States Code as recorded in the Federal Registry, Uniform Commercial Code,

California Penal Code, etc. Through this process, Chris has become a Juris Doctor in Sovereignty Law, Common Law, and Constitutional, Commercial, and Admiralty laws; and has created a business trust for himself. Hereafter he is to be addressed as "Esquire."*

*Not Esquire. That is a Title of Nobility supposedly not allowed by the United States Constitution. It should be noted that the Crown/Bar controls most if not all "legal" systems. Where is the People's Court, a Court based in Law and the sovereignty of each and every man and woman?

And Elsie!* Dear joyous Elsie! She has stuck with us through what I feel is an unpleasant ordeal for her. Never complaining or becoming dispirited and being always very willing and helpful.

*Elsie was my father's secretary and bookkeeper for over thirty years. She later served as trustee.

And I must mention Captain Dave Fuller,* a retired colleague who I did not know and still have never met. He flew aboard out of nowhere like a golden plover coming aboard a vessel at sea, not knowing it was scheduled by pirates to be robbed and shipwrecked. His council has been invaluable.

*My father and I finally did meet Dave Fuller at a United Retired Pilots dinner in San Francisco in 1996. We had a great time.

We are going to prevail over the IRS in this travail. To God be the glory and to Chris, Elsie, and Dave go the credit for a good job well done. Daily I thank the Lord for them. All this has allowed me some free time to pursue my current avocation. I am leading a devotional class of 15 ladies at the Manna Home for battered women, which is a division of the Redwood Gospel Mission.* I also teach a weekly Bible class of men at the Rescue Mission. What a privilege it is to be able to do something useful.

Love and hugs,

Stan

*Coincidentally, during my financial collapse in June, 2018, I stayed at the Redwood Gospel Mission a number of times.

Dear Chris,   1996

   What a sweet and delightful letter you wrote to your Dad. You have always been very thoughtful and communicative. I really do appreciate you more than perhaps I have ever been able to communicate to you. And how understanding is your knowledge. Your discernment of fatherly love is unusual for one your age.

   Nevertheless, you are the one who is standing by Mom and Dad. And while I used to dream of helping all of my sons in attaining good business success and in obtaining the best and most fruitful financial remuneration for the time and effort spent, you are the only one who seems interested enough to listen.*

Love Dad

*My brother Marc has been very supportive to me over the years.

Happy Birthday, Chris   August 31, 1996

   This is written to convey how much I enjoy our evening visits—when you come up and we talk about current events   including: economics and politics and quite a little bit of philosophy. We relate items we have read and we share books and newsletters we each may be currently reading. I think this is great fun as well as intellectually stimulating and do so enjoy these sessions. Without you, how could I have this pleasure? No other man I know has your widespread readership.

Readers are leaders

"Those who won't read are no different from those who can't read.

"Some books leave us free and some make us free." Emerson

The right books could win back most of our freedoms.

Why don't you write it?

In the interim while I am waiting for you to write something that people understand* and that people want to read. I love you and I really enjoy our fellowship. It produces the best kind of kindred relationship.

Love Dad

*My father initially had a difficult time understanding the two-force universe of Man and Woman Balance. Like most, he didn't have a context for it. That began to change during his last months.

Merry Christmas, Chris   December 25, 1996

Being I have the bread machine,* I hope you can find time next summer to use this dryer. You can dry all kinds of vegetables and fruits in it, and even make yogurt. I know that such occupation adds another item to your busy schedule, but practical hobbies of experimentation can be fun and relaxing. I'm having fun from baking bread and muffins.

Love Dad

*My father began to bake bread the last couple of years of his life. He really enjoyed it. He taught me how to bake bread in what turned out to be the last loaf he ever made.

Ron, May 18, 1998

    Bingo! A Victory! A Big Win! A Miracle!—Clear Title in one day.*
New title report came in the mail today. I am faxing over the letter
and pertinent pages. I have mailed the whole report to you. Needless
to say, we are very pleased.

Thank you,

Chris

*This is in reference to the letter I sent to Ron MacDonald after we
received word that the IRS lien was cleared off the title report on Lot 5.
Ron had sent to the Title Company his letter challenging their position
just the day before. When we received word of this, my father was so
happy that for three days he kept saying, "It's a miracle; it's a miracle."
Clear title freed my father from the IRS (Nation-State).

Dad's Prayer 1998

A Prayer

    "We are here to seek the face of Him who alone has been our
help in ages past and is our only hope in days to come.

    "Oh Lord, our Lord, how excellent is thy name in all the earth. We
glory in your handiwork, oh God; towering mountains, deep valleys,
dense forests, expansive deserts, fathomless depth of blue below,
immeasurable heights of blue above.

    "When we peer into our universe with the telescope and your
universe with the microscope, we stand in awe of the complexity
and the simplicity, the order and the chaos, the infinite variety of
designs and colors everywhere.

    "Oh Lord God, creator of the hummingbird and the Milky Way,
we are lost in wonder at your originality.

"Accept our kind offices to your other children as the only means in our power to return a tiny portion of your love.

"We ask this in the name of your son, the living Savior, Jesus Christ."

Amen.*

*My father wrote this prayer in early 1998. I am not sure he wasn't quoting someone. In any event, it was his last written prayer. It was read at his Memorial Service.

June, 1998*

*My father wrote this in early June, 1998 shortly before his appointment with the neurologist, after which we found out my father's had a brain tumor. At this time his writing is hardly legible.

July 12, 1998

Stan Anderson* has been a pioneer in two areas where we shared a close bond. First Stan, you were an aviation pioneer before your retirement, flying everything, the DC-3 through the 747. You made the transition for guys like me much easier. Props to jets was like the stone age to the space age. I guess we have to be satisfied ending up on jets, we're both too old for space.

Next Stan, we transitioned from fear to knowledge. In the late 1980's and early 90's we shared a feeling of terror when the IRS came intruding in our lives. Slowly and then quite rapidly we came to realize that this criminal group could only prey on the people who refused to learn the truth. We learned the truth together and now we are free. Free of fear and free to tell them to go to hell.

I thank you for the very memorable time at the RUPA "boys night out" a couple of years ago. It was a great two days. To meet your family and especially Chris, so now I can put a face on that voice that I've spoken with so often. Hopefully Chris and I can create a little mischief for our intrusive friends in the years to come.

Our bond will not be forgotten Stan.

God speed my friend,

Dave

*From Dave Fuller writing to my father after I told him of my father's diagnosis. I told Dave that if he wanted to say anything to Stan that he had better say it now. I read Dave's letter to my Dad.

Chris, August 2, 1998

I was fine this morning until I heard you speak of your closeness with your Dad.* When you told me that you stayed with him all night, and that he would mumble meaningful phrases, that you responded with, "It's okay, poppa," I could not hold back my emotions. You couldn't have been more piercing had you, with aim, touched my naked emanation, the source of me. I attempted not to speak further with you, so that I could gather my thoughts, and then act confident in my steadfastness. However, all that resounded within me, from then on, was the heartbreak of one man, whom being burdened in the moment with life and death, patiently waits for the demise of his beloved father. My sadness has gathered around me for you, and my prayers are for you, your beloved mother, father, and brothers, that peace and joy be within your hearts as the time dwindles to its end of use in this life for your father.

God Bless,

Ron

*From Ron MacDonald, one week before my father's passing.

Dear Chris;   August 14, 1998

You have lightened my load, and I thank you.* Rarely do a few days go by where I don't think about Stan and his last audit. During the audit I seemed to have been paralyzed, and I was ineffectual in getting rid of Arlo. You, Stan, and I tried so many ways to end the audit, and nothing worked. This has bothered me for years.

During the IRS investigations of last year, I wrote Senator Bill Archer. Without naming names, I described in detail the torment of having audits lasting years, and the destruction of personal lives that followed.

Your talk sounded like a partial victory was achieved after Stan said "enough."

I liked Stan a lot. He was a complex person who made a difference in this world.

If, as the years pass, something comes up and you want to "shoot the breeze," just call.

Sincerely,

GH

*I received this letter shortly after my father's memorial service from our ex-CPA. He had come to the service and heard me speak about my Dad.

Ron, August 22, 1998

Bread

My Dad taught me how to bake bread. He showed me with the last loaf he ever made. In that last loaf was his spirit. Now in each loaf I make lies my Dad's spirit. I was having trouble with the bread maker. The timing has been off. Dad had somehow lost the directions and I could not find the store where the bread maker was purchased. I said, forget it; I will get a new one. I am determined to continue to make bread for my Dad as an expression of his love. I was finally able to locate the manufacturer of the machine and they are going to send me new directions. I also got a card in the mail, addressed to Dad, from the store where the bread maker was bought. I now know that, one way or another, I will be able to make my Dad's bread.

Chris

Press On! *

Nothing in the world can take the place of persistence. Talent will not; nothing is more common than unsuccessful men with talent. Genius will not; unrewarded genius is almost a proverb. Education will not; the world is full of educated derelicts. Persistence and determination alone are omnipotent.

*Perhaps the essence of my father's philosophy. If nothing else, this is what he instilled in me. This quote is attributed to Calvin Coolidge, 30th President of the United States of America.

Conclusion

What do you think? Was my Father right in saying "Enough"? What would you have done? The following quote is from Ron MacDonald's book that was published in 2009.

Ronald P. MacDonald and Robert Rowen, M.D.—*They Own It All (Including You!) By Means of Toxic Currency,* 2009

"With the veil of deceit lifted, you have now discovered that you don't own anything. You are using another entity's property in all your contracts. The foundation of liberty is the ownership of property. Without property that is exclusively yours, how can you enter into any sort of contract without the permission of the lien holder? Simply put, you can't.

"Furthermore, your use of FRNs identifies you as a debtor in use of the creditor's property. You, and every contract into which you enter with its property, are subject to its terms and conditions.

"...Within a few years of the gold confiscation and replacement by marked debt notes, came laws of the kind never seen before in America. Roosevelt's New Deal, allegedly for recovery of the Depression, created agency after agency, board after board, license after license. Occupations, which are your common law right to work, suddenly required a license. A license is permission by the state to do that which otherwise would be illegal.

"...How did even marriage come to need state permission by license? Previously it was a holy contract entered into before God in a house of worship. How did the spiritual product of this union, children, need registration with the state? The answer is that we have become the chattel property of some entity (the Federal Reserve Bank), requiring registration and permission.

"...In 1933, the U.S. government went insolvent. It too then became a debtor subject to the creditor. But you weren't told. We the People don't have any idea what the terms and conditions of that Chapter 11 bankruptcy included. But the evidence leaves a clear trail. The government became the agent of collection for the creditor. The debt was dumped on us. We were collectively beguiled into a debtor's status. The creditor worked the terms and conditions through the government. If the creditor did this openly, we would not be beguiled. But the cruelest and most unconscionable effect from this act is that it is perpetual!"

"*...it is perpetual!*" Debt—It is perpetual. Let us just say that the size of Government is inversely proportional to the prosperity of the people. Or shall we say, the size of Government is proportional to the debt and despair of the people. We don't have unalienable rights today, only privileges. We are not the sovereign; we are the slave. How do I know this? Simple, if **We the People** were the sovereign than we wouldn't have a FED or IRS (or most all of the three letter agencies) that comprise the Administrative State! A FED and IRS are unconstitutional. A Constitution for **We the People** cannot LIVE if it is not premised in the Balance between Man and Woman—which connectively results in *Unalienable Rights for all*!

The following is a recent letter I wrote to Ronna McDaniel, Chairwoman the Republican National Committee.

Ronna McDaniel,*   2/9/24

Thank you for including me in your district canvass. I have filled out the form and am returning it with this cover letter. I hope it finds its way to you.

I am writing this letter because I believe you have left out perhaps the three most important issues concerning one's vote in the upcoming election.

The requirement for a balanced budget. When was the last time Congress balanced its budget? Should that not be foremost for the functional working of government on all levels. Why do certain people/elected officials get to spend what they do not have, placing us all in debt/bondage?

Sound substance money. Today our money is a note (Federal Reserve Note). Doesn't a note have a creditor and a debtor? It appears the FED is the creditor and the American people are the debtor. That means for every dollar printed the American people are obligated to pay it back with interest. Moreover, the FED can basically print all the "money" it wants. It has no backing as in gold or silver. It is created from nothing and "We the People" are required to pay it back with interest. Why does the FED have a monopoly on printing worthless dollars? Isn't that the question? If we do not begin from sound money, as our founding fathers believed in, we might as well forget all these other items as listed on your canvass document.

And what about the IRS, the enforcement arm of the FED? Initially the IRS was sent up to collect corporate taxes. The individual SOVEREIGN people were not to have a corporate tax placed upon them. We the People were, and hopefully still are, the SOVEREIGN. Or were we also somehow turned into corporate entities? Now, it appears we live in a monetary gulag. When it comes to money, we have no rights. So, who is the SOVEREIGN? Do the (Rino) Republicans ever stand up for the SOVEREIGNTY of the people? I think not.

Perhaps the Republican Party would, or certainly should, address these issues. Unless, or until, they are addressed, we will not get our freedom/country back.

Thank you for your time and consideration.

Christopher Anderson

*I did receive a response back but there wasn't any mention of the issues I raised. Moreover, since this letter was written I have heard that Ronna

McDaniel is no longer head of the RNC but has moved on to be a reporter for the main stream press.

Let's return to Ron's quote. He states: *"How did the spiritual product of this union, children, need registration with the state?"* This may be more important than the money issue. It appears that the State requirement of registration/license of marriage and children voids the true spiritual nature of marriage and children. It is shocking to learn that the Nation State's license requirement regarding marriage creates a third party to the "marriage," in this case government. Yesterday, it was the Church as the third party, today it is the State. (And I am not against witnesses to a marriage but that marriage itself is constituted as between one man and one woman, no intermediary.) Today, the State's control includes any children a couple may have as well. Your children are no longer your children!*

*Check out the power of Child Protective Services who can take your child away from you at their, and a Judge's, discretion. Afterall, the State knows best, right?

Let me introduce one more example here of the corporate nation (surveillance) state. This is the Debt Collection Letter. I have provided an example below taking out the names associated. Have you ever received one? I have.* So did Robert. Robert first introduced me to this type of response. Over the years I have simplified it. The key is to not engage. They assume you are already engaged with them, i.e., under their jurisdiction. You are not. The whole government has been co-opted into the one global counterfeit money scam. I must advise, do your own research. Before you respond to any such letter, you must be able make it your own. Don't depend on me. Hopefully, we will be in a gold-backed honest money system shortly. Shortly, is that months or years? I don't know.

*I did have a financial collapse in 2018.

June 27, 2024

Name of Debt Collector

Address

RE: Debt Collection Letter from (Name of Debt Collector) dated (date on letter)

To Whom It May Concern,

This letter is in response to a letter I received on (date received) from (Name of Debt Collector). (See enclosure).

As concerns this letter from (Name of Debt Collector), I am perplexed. I have never had any contact with (Name of Debt Collector). As such, I am returning the letter back to (Name of Debt Collector), having checked no boxes so as not to certify the legitimacy of the (Name of Debt Collector) letter.

Also, your letter makes reference to (Account or Reference #) listed on letter). That is not mine. I do not have an account/reference # with (Name of Debt Collector). I have never purchased a good or service from (Name of Debt Collector).

Furthermore, regarding your instruction to "Call or write by (date listed on letter) to dispute all or part of the debt. If you do not, we will assume that our information is correct." (Name of Debt Collector) does not have a right to give me a time table to respond to their letter on their terms, implying, barring my timely response, that I have some account or linkage or debt with (Name of Debt Collector) in anyway. I do not.*

Lastly, there isn't any signature on the letter dated (date listed on letter) sent to me by (Name of Debt Collector). The letter (Name of Debt Collector) is not properly/legally signed by an authorized representative of (Name of Debt Collector). In fact, this letter from (Name of Debt Collector) is not signed at all. That alone nullifies the legality of said of letter, rendering it void.

Sincerely,

Your name

*Nevertheless, I suggest you respond in the time given.

Now, you might be wondering why I would include a Debt-Collector letter example in a book about Spiritual Procreation. Isn't that somewhat small of me? I mean if I, or you, have a debt should not we pay it back. Well, I remember during the IRS years, it was one of the first letters I received from the IRS. The caption read: Department of Treasury. That's all. Now, let me ask, whose Department of Treasury is that? Could you or I send out a letter to most anyone demanding money with a caption that read Department of Treasury? I think not. Can anyone send you a Debt Collection letter claiming you own some debt and that you need/must pay them. Oh, and the letter has no signature! And it implies you have an account with them? Really! I could go on. The point here is that our money system is fraudulent. It is based on thievery. And the government is the real debt collector. It has us all in debt. That is its (corporate) job.

Now, I know it is very difficult to comprehend that the purpose of the Nation-State (also called the Counterfeit Money Matrix or Global Money Cabal) is simple; it is simply to get rid of our Constitution, especially its first two amendments—the freedom of speech and the right to bear arms—to control us and perhaps even lock us up for "wrong think," i.e., "hate speech," which they, of course, get to define. This is already happening in other countries—and here as well. I hate to say it but it appears we are now living in a surveillance state whose purpose is the control of your pocket book/bank account—oh, and the control of your medical decisions, voting decisions, and religious affiliation, etc. And let's not forget, the State's purpose is also the destruction of the **two-parent man and woman family unit**—the only family unit there is and which is the basis of our **Lives and Sovereigncy**. Each one of us must make the sound decision for substance value-backed money, the two (equal and opposite) parent/family unit, and the sovereign right to earn and own. Can you see that money, family, and freedom are all tied in together? So please, review the beginning quotes to this chapter: And let us add one more.

Stanley Maynard Anderson (1919-1998)—Father

   "Enough!"

O Light Eternal:
The Message of Eternal Life

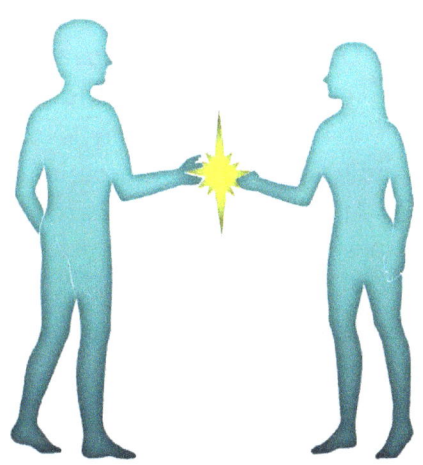

Preface

I have felt for a long time that I was in communication with someone. Not physically but spiritually. One of my first writings published in/around 1985 is titled: *To Cassandra: Early Years*. Here is a selection.

To Cassandra—Early Years © 1985, 1994

I, Cassandra, Will Come

Do not despair, my love
I, Cassandra, will come
To you very shortly.
I know you have waited patiently
And worked so very hard
To show us the way
Out of the impasse
Of our own cosmic blunder.
Yes, I will come soon
(Are you calling for me now?)
And when we unite,
The world will then know
The way into the light.

You see, without that "other" coming to us, or more correctly stated, living in our very hearts/souls, I doubt that we will make any headway towards peace and love both personally and collectively. It is my sincerest hope that this writing, along with my other writings, will serve as a guide to which you and I, and everyone, may find the self-other balance, not just within ourselves but in our (equal and opposite) Eternal Other Half.

To Cassandra—Early Years © 1985, 1994

I Climb the Dark Mountain

I climb the dark mountain
That hasn't any light
To guide me

To its top
Where all can be seen.
Yes, it is a slow climb
I must feel my way
There are no signposts
For me to tell
If I am going
In the right direction
For around me
All is dark.
Pitch black
But don't look back
For with one misstep
I may lose my feel
For what is real
And then all would be lost
Without any light
To guide me
Through the dark night.

"I believe in us."

Christopher Alan Anderson
August 31, 1950 –

Contents

O Light Eternal

God is Life

The Eternal and The Procreative are One

The Eternal Process of Male and Female Division and Unification

A Philosophical Structure

A New Trinity for Spiritual Healing

The Holy Spirit Has Come

Our Eternal Life Together

O Light Eternal

Martin Heidegger (1888-1976)—German philosopher

"The mystery is that there is something rather than nothing."

Does something really exist? Is something the "metaphysical given"? But what about no-thing? Aren't things just an illusion? Separate and apart. Perhaps in back of the something is a "grand nothingness." Why are so many of us afraid of death? Perhaps it is because we are afraid of our own *nothingness*. Does not death spell the eternal end of ourselves—and our loved ones too? Someone once said, *"If God did not exist, it would be necessary to invent Him."* Perhaps it was Voltaire. Why would it be necessary to invent God? Is it because we are afraid of our own extinction? Does not God promise to us Eternal Life? Well, in Christianity, the religion of my upbringing, it states *"For God so loved the world, that he gave his only begotten Son, that whosoever believeth in him should not perish, but have everlasting life."* (John 3:16) Let's continue: 17) *"For God sent not his Son into the world to condemn the world; but that the world through him might be saved."* 18) *"He that believeth on him is not condemned: but he that believeth not is condemned already, because he hath not believed in the name of the only begotten Son of God."* 19) *"And this is the condemnation. That light is come into the world, and men loved darkness rather than light, because their deeds were evil."* 20) *"For everyone that doeth evil hateth the light, neither cometh to the light, lest his deeds should be reproved."* 21) *"But he that doeth truth cometh to the light, that his deeds may be made manifest, that they are wrought in God."*

It may be worthwhile to notice both the terms *light* and *truth* are included herein. I would like to suggest here that the term *light* does not just mean physical light but actually has a spiritual connotation. We might think of the spiritual light as existing before/behind the physical light—*A light behind the light.*

Charles Williams (1886 – 1945)—British poet and novelist.

"A light that shone from behind the sun; the sun was not so fierce as to pierce where that light could."

Here are a few more quotes on "the Light."

Dante Alighieri (1265-1321)—*The Divine Comedy, Paradiso, Canto, XXXIII*

"Eternal Light, you only dwell within Yourself, and only You know you, Self-knowing, Self-known, You love and smile upon Yourself! That circle—which, begotten so, appeared in You as light reflected—when my eyes had watched it with attention in You as light reflected—when my eyes had watched it with attention for some time, within itself and colored like itself, to me seemed painted with our effigy, so that my sight was set on it completely. As the geometer intently seeks to square the circle, but he cannot reach, through thought on thought, the principle he needs, so I search that strange sight: I wished to see the way in which our human effigy suited the circle and found place in it—and my own wings were far too weak for that. But then my mind was struck by light that flashed and, with this light, received what it has asked. Here force failed my high fantasy; but my desire and will were moved already—like a wheel revolving uniformly—*by the Love that moves the sun and the other stars.*"

Walter Russell (1871-1963)—*The Universal One* 1926

"Light, as man knows the light is but an unstable simulation of the real light of the Universal One. Man's concept of light is luminosity, an illusion of the universal light of inertia, sustained in its appearance as an illusion of light by the pressures generated through motion. The inner mind of ecstatic man knows the real light and that he is one with the light. He is not deceived by its illusion."

Walt Whitman (1819 – 1892) *Leaves of Grass: Song for Myself* (First Edition) 1855

"I swear I see now that everything has an eternal soul! The trees have, rooted in the ground....the weeds of the sea have....the animals.

"I swear I think there is nothing but immortality! That the

exquisite scheme is for it, and the nebulous float is for it, and the cohering is for it, And all preparation is for it...the identity is for it, and life and death are for it."

Dante uses the term, *Eternal Light*. Walter Russell uses the term *Light* equating it to *The Universal One*. Walt Whitman uses the term, *Eternal Soul*. Might there be other terms for the Light behind the light? Certainly, the term *God* must be included. How about *Soul* or *Spirit*? A philosophical term may be the *Metaphysical Given, the What Is, a something rather than nothing.* We just can't begin any inquiry into anything without stipulating a *something rather than nothing*. There isn't a metaphysical nothing. **Nothingness does not exist.**

But I wonder, can any of this be proven? Here is where we get into some sticky waters. The Metaphysical Given, as it were, cannot be proven. It is the beginning point of what must be accepted for there to be proof. The novelist and Objectivist philosopher Ayn Rand begins her philosophy on the axiom (a statement accepted as true) *existence exists*. We don't really prove that, do we? We just must <u>accept</u> it. It is a given/starting point. Proof comes from that, not to that.

Well, I wonder, if there isn't a Metaphysical Given per se then can anything be claimed to be the Metaphysical Given? Can we begin from 2 + 2 = 5? How about from **God is**? Is that so just because we might want it to be so? What about for every action there must be and equal and opposite reaction? Science seeks proof. Religion claims God is supernatural, not just beyond proof but beyond our conceptual understanding. It seems mankind has been seeking some certainty within him or herself regarding this fundament issue since day one. At stake, I believe, is our own sanity—and survival. How do we get through the death/extinction barrier? Is the Void/Abyss the best we can hope for? What is the answer? Is there an answer?

I believe there is. The answer lies in that there is something rather than nothing, i.e. existence exists. Right now, for example, I am certain that *I exist*. Moreover, I am also certain that **You exist.**

In short, ***I am and You are.*** Deny this if you want. Denial just proves it. (We are taking a simple step beyond Descartes', *"I think therefore I am."*) Just this one simple idea brings something into our lives. That something is called **Balance.** There is a fundamental balance between you and I. Moreover, it brings something into our hearts. This other something is called **Love.** May we conclude that balance and love are also primary to our existence? Well, there is something rather than nothing. I am suggesting that this something is the **Spiritual Light of Balance** resulting in a **Love** between You and I. ***I am and You are.***

Genesis 1:3: *And God said, Let there be light: and there was light.*

God is light. God did not create light. God and light are one. Light was never created and can never be destroyed. I speak here of the light behind the light, *the real light of the Universal One.* The real light of the Universal One is that something exists rather than nothing. And it exists in each one of us right now. It is the substance of our very beings. It is held in place by our balance together and expressed in our love, one to another.

Genesis 1:27: *So God created man in his own image, in the image of God created he him, male and female created he them.*

We exist together in the image of God which is **Balance**. Walter Russell states it this way.

Walter Russell (1871-1963)—*The Universal One* 1926
"In the beginning, God. There is but one God. There is but one universe. God is the universe. God is not one and the universe another. The universe is not a separate creation of God's. It is God. There is no created universe. Nothing is which has not always been... Man conceives a perfect and omnipotent God. A perfect and omnipotent God could not create imperfection. He could not create a lesser than Himself. He could not create a greater than Himself. God could not create other than Himself. God did not create other than Himself, nor greater, nor lesser than Himself."

God's love and your love are the same love. God's love and my love are also the same love. This is to say that love does not have a different nature, one for God and another for You or I. Love is love. It lies deep within our hearts/souls. Our very thought/expression is imprinted/encoded in love as per the balance. Let's take this in.

God is Life

There is another term we may use for God, and that is *Life*. Life is. Life is the "what is," the eternal Metaphysical Given. Life is not created. Life does have a **Principle** and **Process** as it were but it itself is an eternal absolute. "But, why is there life?" you ask. Because there is! I exist and you exist. Can we deny our own existences?

Peter V. Ross—If A Man Die He Shall Live Again, 1945

"It was never made or created; it always was, it always will be. Its origin cannot be determined, its extinction cannot be conceived, its confines cannot be crossed. For this is a living not a lifeless world. Life not only pervades the universe; it is the universe."

Peter V. Ross—Leaves of Healing: Method of Metaphysical Treatment, 1946

"It is that Light which shineth in darkness, that Light which symbolizes Life. The Life is in you and through you and is all there is to you. There is nothing besides God; no, nothing in you besides His Mind and Life.

"Life is like beauty in that it is not made. It is. The Creator did not cause or put forth Life. The Creator is Life. Bodying forth in you, Life retains its native quality of permanence.

"No individual is sufficient unto himself. The Biblical apothegm, *'It is not good that the man should be alone,'* epitomizes the wisdom of the ages. Says Luther, *'God has set the type of marriage everywhere throughout creation. Each creature seeks its perfection in another. The very heavens and earth picture it to us.'*

"You ask where Principle is. It is in you. You are a perfect blend with it. You and Principle are one. Hence your power to control situations.

"And you are as unbreakable as Principle, of which you are the expression. ...Life (yours) is unlaboredly continuous—omnipotently irrepressible. And you are altogether too important and too indispensable even to be 'laid up.'

"The omnipresence of God means that perfection exists at every point in the universe."

For Mr. Ross (and Dante, Walter Russell, and Walt Whitman) the Universe is a Living Universe. Life undermines all existence. **Life is the Given**. Life was never created and cannot be destroyed. So, the question arises, why Life? Because Life is what is. God is Life. Okay, but how can we prove this and know that we know? Maybe this is where we step into the feeling side of things. Feel life. Feel your own life. Feel the life of another. Each one of us exists in LIFE. And moreover, we do not exist of ourselves alone. We exist hand and hand with one another.

Life

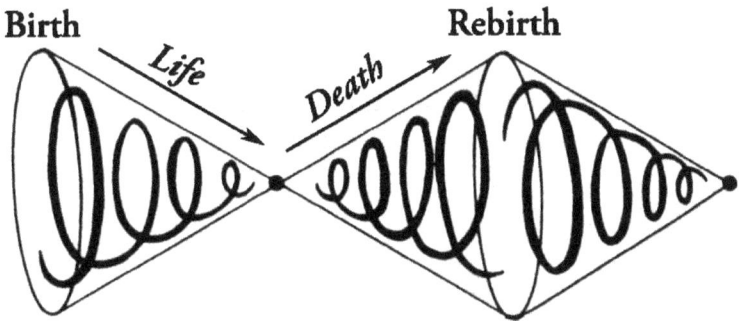

The Eternal and The Procreative are One

Procreation is fundamental to Life! Said another way, the Principle/Process of Life is that of **Procreation**. This is one of the most difficult issues mankind has to face. Heretofore, mankind has not understood that God, what is called the Given or 1st Principle, is not and cannot be separate from Procreation. Let us state that Balance is the 1st Principle and Procreation is its Life Process. It is important to understand that Procreation is not secondary to God/Balance/Life. No, it is the **Living Process** of God/Balance/Life. Let's review some bible verses.

Genesis 1:3: *And God said, Let there be light: and there was light.*

Genesis 1:27: *So God created man in his own image, in the image of God created he him, male and female created he them.*

Genesis 2:24: *Therefore shall a man leave his father and his mother, and shall cleave unto his wife: and they shall be one flesh.*

Matthew 19:4-6: *Have ye not read, that he which made them in the beginning made them male and female, And said, for this cause shall a man leave father and mother, and shall cleave to his wife: and they twain shall be one flesh? Wherefore they are no more twain, but one flesh. What therefore God hath joined together, let not man put asunder.*

Can you capture a sense of this **Procreative Process of Life**?

Webster's New World Dictionary

Balance: *A state of equilibrium or equipoise, equality in amount...as between two things.* **Equilibrium:** *A state of balance or equality between opposing forces.*

Procreant: *Producing young; fruitful. Of procreation.* **Procreate:** *To produce young; beget offspring; reproduce. To produce or bring into existence.*

Procreation, as I am using the term, constitutes the begetting of Life. It is a sexual process of bringing forth new Life. I ask, must not it be part and parcel of the Given? Heretofore, mankind has placed procreation on a 2nd tier under a singular God. What is amazing is that we can't really find the term procreation used in the Bible, at least not as a primary. There is some sense of it, in the verses I have cited, especially in Matthew 19:4-6. *The Dictionary of Philosophy and Religion—Eastern and Western Thought* is talking all around it. But almost nowhere do we see the fundamental inherency/necessity of Procreation existing as the exact **Process of Life**. The **Metaphysical Given of Life** is not some static singular thing somehow outside of or separate from the exact **Procreant Process of Life**.

William L. Reese—*The Dictionary of Philosophy and Religion—Eastern and Western Thought*, 1980

Principle of Polarity

1. *Nicholas of Cusa held that polar opposites apply at the same time to infinite beings. God is the chief example of the principle's applicability.*

2. *Fichte, Hegel, and Marx and his followers believed that such opposites were replaced by a synthesis in the process of dialectic.*

3. *Schelling advanced the idea of a basic polarity in God which was itself a permanent and eternal contrast within God. This point of view was followed by Fechner, Whitehead, Przywara, and Hartshorne.*

4. *According to Morris Cohen the principle of polarity refers to the situation that many analyses require a balancing of two opposing ideas, and that to eliminate either is to run the risk of an inadequate analysis. W.H. Sheldon found the principle important to metaphysical analysis.*

Opposites

Some systems of philosophy have placed a stress on the role of opposites:

1. *The Pythagoreans developed a table of opposites reflecting a basic duality in the universe.*

2. *Heraclitus found a "tension of opposites" providing the order and dynamism of the universe.*

3. *In Taoism Yang and Yin represent opposites in terms of which the universe operates.*

4. *Nicholas of Cusa presented a doctrine called the "coincidence of opposites" which applied to God, the Infinite Being.*

5. *Hegel believed the basic processes of reality and thought moved through contraries into novel unities.*

6. *Gnosis:* The male and female or antithetical (directly opposed) pairs of the first principle.*

*I have added the last definition, No. 6, to this list (although the definition of Gnosis is not my own) that I think better completes *The Dictionary of Philosophy and Religion's* list.

Probably the best articulation I have found comes from the Russell's writings. This one happens to be from Lao Russell, the wife of Walter Russell.

Lao Russell (1904-1988)—*Why You Cannot Die: The Continuity of Life, Reincarnation Explained*, 1972

"Know thou that thou shalt know space, but never emptiness for:

"Behold! I am Space and I fill all of it.

"I am its One, its undivided Father-Mother One of my universe.

"I divide My oneness, and behold! I am two—father and mother.

"These two extend from Me, one on My right hand and one on My left.

"Each equally balanced with the other in the Oneness of their matehood.

"And then, behold! My two become one in Me, the One Father-Mother, undivided—

"To again become two to Father-Mother my eternal universe."

Can you see the Procreative Process in play? Heretofore, we have not viewed the Universal Order/Process as the **Sexual Process of Life**. In short, we have yet to understand the purpose/necessity of the sexes, male and female (Man and Woman), that they themselves comprise the **Universal Process of Life**! The following letter was written to me from my friend Robert Birk to which I dedicate this writing. It is followed by a quote from one of my writings.

Chris   11/8/99

"In your writings, you have defined the TRUE nature of the WORD as being PROCREATIVE and the ONE order, context, process, and structure of the universe, and that MAN and WOMAN are its TWO electrodes of manifesting! Without you having made this connection from the Russell's,* I wouldn't be writing all this down, and there would be no Ruchell** and me, and there would be no "The Secret of Creating the Present Moment."*** The great awakening would still be floundering, waiting for greater definition. This is the second coming as it were. In the name of Ruchell and me, I PROCLAIM it so."

*Walter and Lao Russell, the spiritual mentors for both Robert and myself.

**Robert's wife Ruchell who took care of Robert during his illness. Thank you Ruchell for never giving up on Robert. Your love together is Eternal Love.

***The Secret of Creating the Present Moment was a seminar Robert was working on. Due to health concerns, he was not able to present it.

And from one of my own writings:

...and the TWO shall become as ONE—Encoded in the Book of Eternal Life © 2010; Meditations for Deepening Love © 1994

In the heart of every man and woman, the TWO, is placed the eternal desire to become as ONE. This desire is known as love. "May I give my life to you," the man shouts. "Yes, please do," the woman responds. And out of this love a new birth of life, a new born boy or girl, is brought forth as the eternal desire moves on. The ONE has just become the TWO again. This eternal process is called the *procreant*—a procreative process of balanced interchange between the TWO and the ONE.

And so the TWO becomes as ONE. Not a ONE of no TWO, but a TWO within a ONE for, procreantly, every ONE will again become a TWO. Within the ONE is always the divided TWO. Within the TWO is always the united ONE. And so the 'AS ONE' is actually a BALANCE between the dividing TWO and the uniting ONE. This balance is sexual in that the parts dividing and uniting are opposite pairs, opposite meaning sexual as in male and female pairs. *Sexual balanced interchange* is this procreant and eternal process, the ONE dividing into sexual opposites (the TWO) and the TWO uniting into the sexual equilibrium or rest of the ONE.

Or simply stated:

"And so the TWO becomes as ONE. Not a ONE of no TWO, but a TWO within a ONE for, procreantly, every ONE will again become a TWO. Within the ONE is always the divided TWO. Within the TWO is always the united ONE."

Can you make the distinction that Robert made—*"the TRUE nature of the WORD as being PROCREATIVE and the ONE order, context, process, and structure of the universe, and that MAN and WOMAN are its TWO electrodes of manifesting!"* Or, in short—*a two primary forces*? Or to state from my writing: **"Within the ONE is always the divided TWO. Within the TWO is always the united ONE."**

The Eternal Process of Male and Female Division and Unification

Now, what is the question(s) before us?; the question(s) that to date we have failed to articulate much less answer. Let me give them to you.

What is a man?

What is a woman?*

*Matt Walsh, writer and reporter, brought to the forefront the question, "What is a woman?" in 2023. This question has not yet been answered and cannot be answered until the question, "What is a man?" is equally considered.

What is Male?  What is Female?

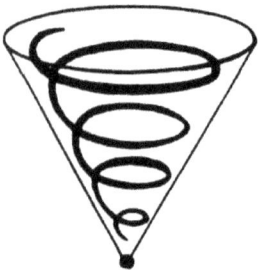 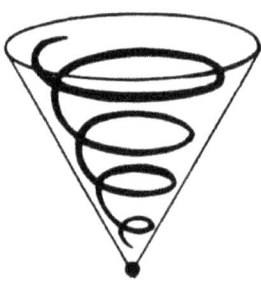

Unless and until we answer these questions, not just intellectually but in feeling within our own hearts and souls, we have nothing. Isn't it about time we truly come to know ourselves in relation to our equal and opposite sexual other half, and equally know our equal and opposite sexual other half as our own completion? How long has mankind been on planet Earth? And we still do not know the sexual necessity of our lives and now we, male and female, need each other as much as we need ourselves. ***One is not without the other; both are need for either to be.***

The Two Forces of Creation © 1988—Selected Writings, Volume 2 © 1991, 2010

Male is that force which seeks to individualize a form separate and apart from the unity of male-female. The male desire is to hold male and female in individual form. It is the active conscious effort of holding separate (sexual) identity in relation to the other. The male effort is simply to hold apart and stabilize the man and woman relationship. We call this the effort to secure individual form or just *security*.

Female is that force which seeks to unite the division of male and female. The female desire is to unite the separate male and female forms together as one. She rests the man and woman relationship through unifying the male within herself. It is from this unity that the next division or reproduction of life can take place. The female effort then is to unite the separate forms of male and female, resting the separate forms in unity so that the next reproduction of sexual form will take place. We call this resting of old form/begetting of new form *reproduction*.

In essence, it is the male effort to secure form and the female effort to reproduce form that makes for life and its continuity. Each aspect makes for one half of their creative process. Yet, and this is an important point, neither aspect can complete their creative desire without the other. The male cannot continually secure form. That effort is fatiguing and brings on a desire to rest. It is at this point that the male takes what he has secured in form and gives it over to female. The male deposits his life seed (force) into a female, releasing his form into her from which his next reproduction, through her, will occur. So without periodic rest or release of form into female, the male cannot continue to fulfill his own desire to secure form.

Likewise, the female cannot continually rest/reproduce form. She herself must sequentially effort, and does so equal to male in preparing herself to receive male as well as nurturing new form. In this fashion, she supports the securing effort of male which also secures herself. Female is actually called to surrender her life to the male desire to individualize form even though her primary desire is to unite, for without that division of the one into two there would not be the two sexual selves to unite. Conversely, at this point of unity, the male is called to surrender his life to the female desire to unite the forms even though his primary desire is to individualize.

Without the unity of the two into one, there would not be a unified one from which the next division of male and female can occur.

It is important to understand the equality of the two opposite forces of male and female. They each operate under different desires and yet both are equally essential for either of them to be. The male force alone or the female force alone is impotent. Without the other neither can be. They need each other. Each is as important to the other as they are to themselves. Both are called upon to make the ultimate surrender of their lives to the other. Neither is ever without the other. Both always are. *Male and female, the two forces of creation, are what is.*

The Sexual Process

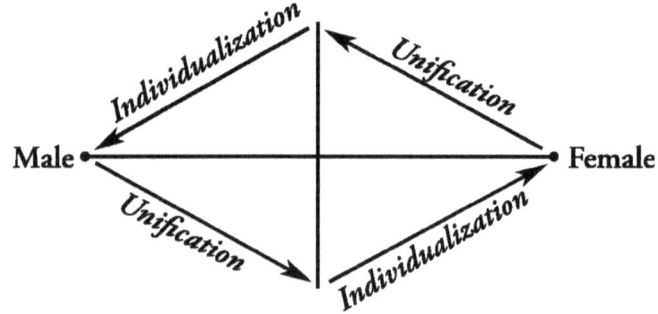

Who am "I"?

I am a male in relationship to a female,
or
I am a female in relationship to a male

. . . whichever sexuality "I" happen to be,

"You" being the sexual opposite of me.

And they look into each other's eyes knowing for all time:

Why am "I" here?

"I" am here to express the sexuality that "I" am . . .

-Male, being that force which seeks to individualize a form separate and apart from the unity of male-female.

-Female, being that force which seeks to unite separate forms together from the division of male and female.

. . . so that together we may continue to manifest

our own sexual creation.

A man and a woman meet and a miracle occurs—a new life is formed. The miracle of life is held within their balance and love. Life, all of life, is held within their balance and love.

The Man and Woman Relationship

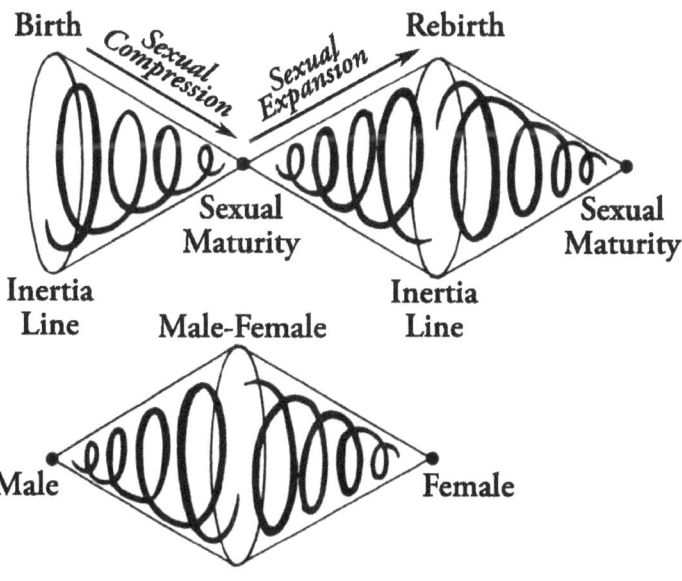

The Discovery of Life © 1994

Male, then, is that force that divides the one. Female is that force which unites the two. This creative or sexual distinction is the great discovery of life and requires a deep comprehension. There just isn't anything else in all of creation but the two opposite forces of male and female, dividing and uniting together, each under the direction of their unique and opposite sexual purpose. You see, there isn't anything more real to life than a male and a female. Life is composed of these two forces. This is life, right now. We are all riding the universal wave of creation. Think of it as an ocean and the male and female forces as a ship. Male is the motor. The male purpose is to power it (divide the one and initiate action). Female is the rudder. It is her purpose to guide the ship (unite the two and complete the action in reaction.) We can never get off this ship for it is the vessel of the universe. We can only try and sail as straight a course as possible.

...To be conscious then is to be sexually conscious. The monotheistic (one-force) consciousness does not present us with sexual consciousness for the two forces are not identified essentially in creation. We just are not, and cannot be, fully conscious without the recognition of our sexual self in relationship to our sexual opposite.

...And now we can return to the question, Who am 'I'? including an added question, Why am 'I' here? These two questions are the fundamental questions of our sexual identities and realities.

The Two Forces of Creation © 1988—Selected Writings, Volume 2 © 1991, 2010

The two faces of love are reflected in a male and a female. Each of these faces is different from the other, yet they each convey one of the two aspects of love. The two aspects of love are male individualization and female unification in interaction together. Love is male and female in rhythmic balanced interchange.

The face of a man reveals his stand, holding the division of male and female secure in creation. A man's face reflects the depth of his stand and shows his capacity to love. The face of a woman reveals her stand, holding the unity of male-female within herself from which the next division of creation will occur. A woman's face also reflects the depth of her stand in showing her capacity to love.

The depth of their love together will be dependent on the knowledge they hold of their sexual essence from which they then act. The key to love and the capacity to surrender lies in the two distinct sexual essences of male and female and our knowledge (consciousness) of that.

And to repeat a passage from ***A Love Perfected: The Coming Age of Sexual Procreation***.

And finally, with this understanding of our universal (equal but opposite) sexuality, let us begin to behold a living universe of spiritual procreation centered on the balance of a man and a woman which simply is their love together.

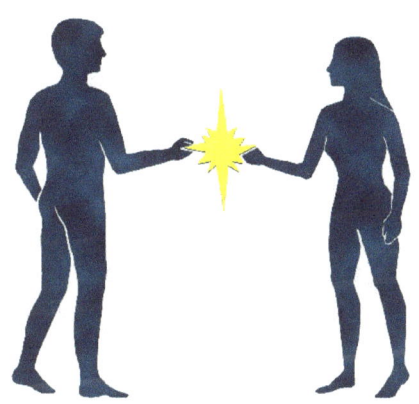

A Philosophical Structure

In this chapter we will review a Philosophical Structure, mostly through pictures and diagrams. There is crossover here with the *A Love Perfected: The Coming Age of Spiritual Procreation*. Both *O Light Eternal: The Message of Eternal Life* and *A Love Perfected: The Coming Age of Spiritual Procreation* were written over the course of a period of 10+ years back in the early 2000s.

Paul Strathern—*Socrates in 90 Minutes*

"It has taken philosophers twenty-five centuries of getting it wrong to conclude that getting it wrong isn't the point. Now they believe that the mere practice of philosophy is what matters. Thus, philosophy has become an activity, like wine-tasting or tax evasion, with similarly ambiguous effects on the practitioner. For the first time in the history of philosophy, the attempt by any individual to construct a philosophy as such has become redundant. The tradition of Plato, Kant, Ehrensvard, and Wittgenstein has come to an end. This tradition of reason and observation, which attracted some of the finest minds the world has known, first grew to maturity with Socrates."

A Truth Model

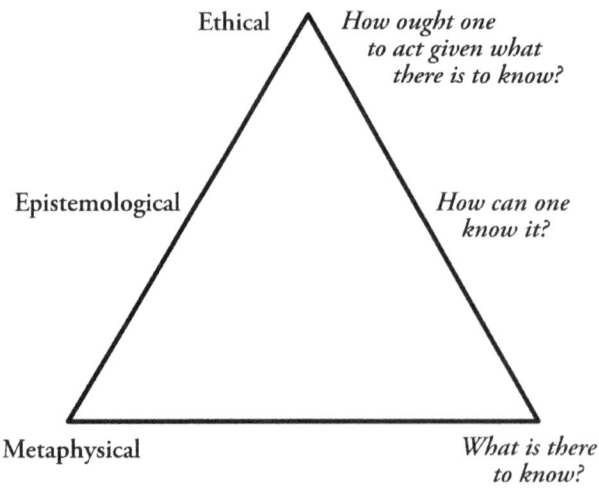

	Absolute	**Relativity**
Metaphysics	*Reality*	*Illusion*
Epistemology	*Certainty*	*Skepticism/Opinion*
Ethics	*Morality*	*License*

The Evolution of Consciousness

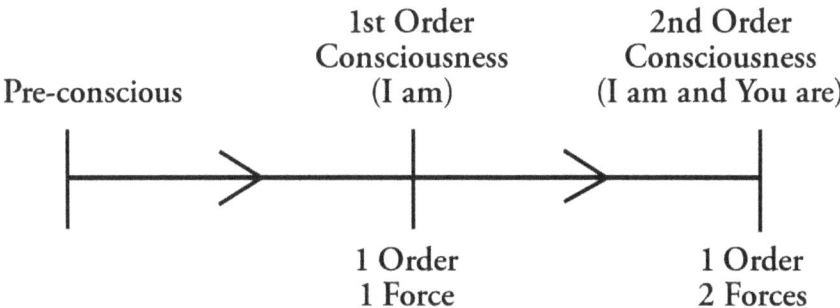

Equal and Opposite

The Old Testament of the Holy Bible, King James Version Genesis 1:27: *So God created man in his own image, in the image of God created he him, male and female created he them.*

Genesis 6:19: *And of every living thing of all flesh, two of every sort shalt thou bring into the ark, to keep them alive with thee; they shall be male and female.*

The New Testament of the Holy Bible, King James Version Matthew 19:4-6: *Have ye not read, that he which made them in the beginning made them male and female, And said, for this cause shall a man leave father and mother, and shall cleave to his wife: and they twain shall be one flesh? Wherefore they are no more twain, but one flesh. What therefore God hath joined together, let not man put asunder.*

The Koran
51:49: *And all things We have made in pairs, so that you may give thought.*

Socrates (470-400 B.C.)—*Protagoras*
"Everything has one opposite and not more than one."

Socrates—*Philebus*
"The one and the many become identified by thought…This union of them never cease, and is not now beginning, but is…an everlasting quality of thought itself, which never grows old."

Ralph Waldo Emerson (1803-1882)
"The One, and the Two. 1. Unity or Identity; and 2. Variety. We unite all things by perceiving the law which pervades them. By perceiving the superficial differences, and the profound resemblances. But every mental act,— this very perception of identity or oneness, recognized the difference of things. Oneness and Otherness. It is impossible to speak, or to think without embracing both."

Walter Russell—*The Divine Iliad*, 1948
"For again I say My one principle of My one law is founded upon the solid rock of equal interchange between all pairs of opposite things, opposite conditions, or opposite transactions between men."

Walter and Lao Russell—*Atomic Suicide?*, 1957
"The Father-Mother of Creation divides His sexless unity into sex-divided pairs of father and mother bodies, for the purpose of uniting them to create other pairs of father and mother bodies in eternal sequences forever."

Richard Garnett (1835-1906)
"Man and woman may only enter Paradise hand-in-hand. Together…they left it,, and together they must return."

Walt Whitman—*Leaves of Grass*, 1855
Song for Myself
"I have heard what the talkers were talking….the talk of the beginning and the end,

But I do not talk of the beginning or the end.

There was never any more inception than there is now, Nor any more youth or age than there is now;

And will never be any more perfection than there is now, Nor any more heaven or hell than there is now.

Urge and urge and urge,

Always the procreant urge of the world.

Out of the dimness opposite equals advance…Always substance and increase.

Always a knit of identity….always distinction….always a breed of life."

Walt Whitman—*I Sing the Body Electric*
"This is the nucleus…after the child is born of woman, This is the bath of birth…this is the merge of small and large and the outlet again."

Webster's New World Dictionary
Balance: A state of equilibrium or equipoise, equality in amount…as between two things. **Equilibrium:** A state of balance or equality between opposing forces.

Procreant: Producing young; fruitful. Of procreation. **Procreate:** To produce young; beget offspring; reproduce. To produce or bring into existence.

Structural Balance

(Equal and Opposite)

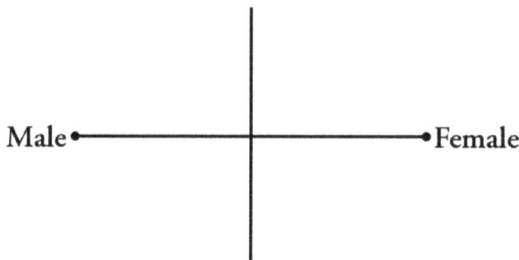

Structural Imbalance

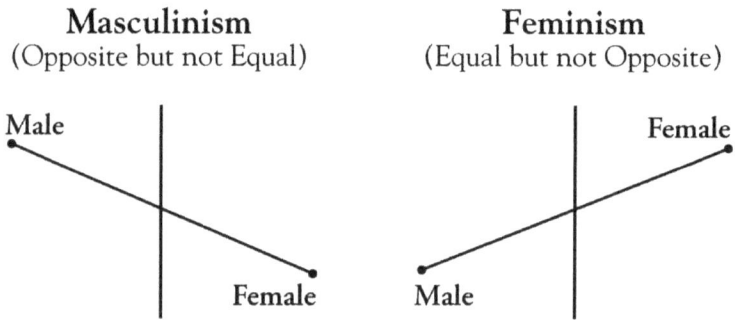

Aristotle's Laws of Logic

The Principle of Identity – A is A or whatever is is what it is.

The Principle of Contradiction – A is not "not A"

or something is what it is and is not what it is not.

The Principle of the Excluded Middle – Everything is either A or "not A" or something cannot be both A and "not A."

Aristotle's Laws of Logic Revised

The Principle of Identity – A is A; B is B.

The Principle of Contradiction – A is not B; B is not A.

The Principle of the Excluded Middle – Everything is either A or B. (What is not A is B and what is not B is A.)

The Principle of Connection* – A is in relation to B; B is in relation to A.

*Hungarian philosopher Akos Van Pauler (1876-1933) suggested that a fourth law be added to the principles of logic which he called the *Law of Connection*.

Aristotle's Laws of Logic Sexed

The Principle of Identity – Male is male; Female is female.

The Principle of Contradiction – Male is not female; Female is not male.

The Principle of the Excluded Middle – Everything is either Male or Female. (What is not Male is female; what is not Female is male.)

The Principle of Connection – Male is in relation to female; Female is in relation to male.

The Choices

Man and Woman Balance	Religious Imbalance	Political Imbalance	Sexual Imbalance
M — S — F	S	S	S
|	|	|	|
M — M — F	M — M — F	M	M
|	|	|	|
M — B — F	M — B — F	M — B — F	B

S — Spirit   M — Mind   B — Body   M — Male   F — Female

The Given

- There is something (not necessarily a thing).

- That this "something" is in relationship.

- There is something else.

- That this "relationship" is metaphysically equal and creativity opposite.

- That this "relationship" is creative and therefore sexual.

- That this "relationship" is the creative process of male and female individualization and unification.

The Essential Proof

Life itself becomes the self-evident "proof" of the given

of the two forces of creation that comprises Life!

Equation for Eternal Life

Given that Man and Woman Balance =

Procreative Love, and Procreative Love =

the Survival of the Species or Perpetual Creation,

and Perpetual Creation = Eternal Life;

thus Man and Woman Balance = Eternal Life

The Universal Axiom of Life

It takes a man and a woman to make a baby!

The Eternal Process of Male and Female Division and Unification

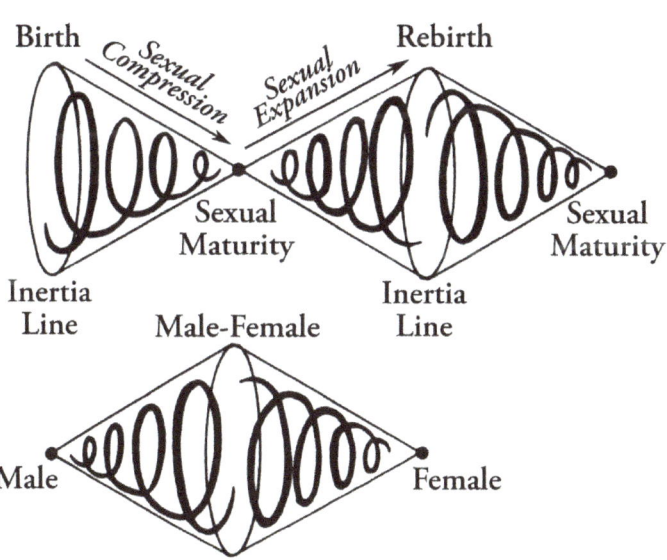

The Alignment Drawings

```
M — S — F         S                S              S
   |              |                |              |
M — M — F     M — M — F            M              M
   |              |                |              |
M — B — F     M — B — F        M — B — F          B
```

S — Spirit   M — Mind   B — Body   M — Male   F — Female

The Eternal and the Procreative Are One

The eternal is that which is procreative to life. This will be our message. Our love is a procreative love. Our lives are procreative together. And as such we know the eternal in our hearts and souls as we reach out to each other in the one touch that is an eternal touch. With this said, let me bring to your attention again *The Eternal Prayer*. *The Eternal Prayer* contains the spirit that comprises the light that is the touch, one sexual soul to another, now and forevermore.

The Eternal Prayer

My blessed love, please come into my heart and live in me. Allow me, as well, to come into your heat and live in you. Let us, from this moment on, live in each other's hearts, our love together being our guide, shining a light for all to see that life is held simply in our balance together.

From the poem *Touch, To Cassandra—Early Years*. The last stanza reads:

>   Cassandra
>   Shall you and I
>   Walk into our silence
>   Together
>   Down the aisle
>   Arm and arm
>   Into the abyss
>   Forever
>   To only return
>   When called desire
>   Between a man and woman
>   To touch.

Our love, that is the love between a man and a woman, is eternal love. Our life together is simply an expression of *our eternal love*. The whole universe of life is an expression of *our eternal love*. Eternal love is eternal life. *Eternal life*, what an interesting idea, brought to consciousness by a simple abstraction between a *one* order and a *two* forces.*

*All philosophy, to be credible, from this moment on, *must* be an expression of love, expressed from one to his or her (equal and opposite) other half!

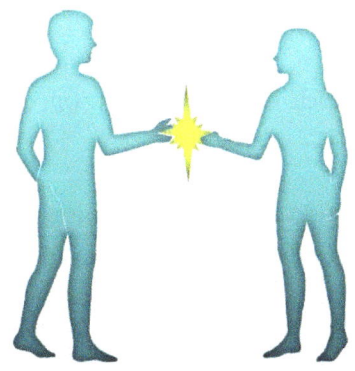

Our love is eternal love!

A New Trinity for Spiritual Healing

I was brought up into a Christian home. (John 3:16 was the verse of one's salvation.) The question/issue that heretofore has never been adequately answered is: "Who comes first." According to the Christian doctrine, Jesus (as the supposedly one and only Son of God) comes first. We are required to accept Jesus into our hearts as our personal savior to be saved. Would anyone do this if he or she did not believe that he or she would be given eternal life? In other words, we only do this for our own interests, our own salvation. It really comes down to ME first and you second. What, I wonder, holds Jesus in this deified status? Remember the Walter Russell quotes:

Walter Russell (1871-1963) *The Universal One,* **1926**
"In the beginning, God. There is but one God. There is but one universe. God is the universe. God is not one and the universe another. The universe is not a separate creation of God's. It is God. There is no created universe. Nothing is which has not always been... Man conceives a perfect and omnipotent God. A perfect and omnipotent God could not create imperfection. He could not create a lesser than Himself. He could not create a greater than Himself. God could not create other than Himself. God did not create other than Himself, nor greater, nor lesser than Himself."

Walter Russell (1871-1963) *The Divine Iliad*, **1948**
"For again I say My one principle of My one law is founded upon the solid rock of equal interchange between all pairs of opposite things, opposite conditions, or opposite transactions between men."

Walter and Lao Russell - *Atomic Suicide?* **1957**
"The Father-Mother of Creation divides His sexless unity into sex-divided pairs of father and mother bodies, for the purpose of uniting them to create other pairs of father and mother bodies in eternal sequences forever."

Might I suggest that it is not just the crucifixion and resurrection that hold Jesus in deified status. Perhaps it is the Virgin Birth that holds the whole Christian religion together.

Christ's Virgin Birth (Author Unknown)

"The virgin birth is an underlying assumption in everything the Bible says about Jesus. To throw out the virgin birth is to reject Christ's deity, the accuracy and authority of Scripture, and a host of other related doctrines that are the heart of the Christian faith. No issue is more important than the virgin birth to our understanding of who Jesus is. If we deny that Jesus is God, we have denied the very essence of Christianity. Everything else the bible teaches about Christ hinges on the truth we celebrate at Christmas—that Jesus is God in human flesh. If the story of His birth is merely a fabricated or trumped-up legend, then so is the rest of what Scripture tells us about Him. The virgin birth is as crucial as the resurrection in substantiating His deity. It is not an optional truth. Anyone who rejects Christ's deity rejects Christ absolutely—even if he pretends otherwise."

There is another term that quite adequately ties the Virgin Birth and Christ's crucifixion and resurrection together and that is the Christian Trinity, that God exists as the Father, the Son, and the Holy Spirit. But, I can't help but ask, where is Woman? We are told that Jesus' mother was impregnated by God the Father. Not by her husband Joseph but by God himself. This is to suggest that the process of eternal life is not centered in the act of procreation where the two, man and woman, become as one to create the lineage of life—and a child is born. In the Russell writings they suggest a **New Trinity**, called the **Divine Trinity**.

Walter and Lao Russell—*Atomic Suicide?*, 1957

What the Divine Trinity suggests to us is that there are two primary forces of creation, and they are male and female—***Two Forces***. I remember the day well, my friend Robert Birk was visiting my home. Robert had stopped by as his job at the time brought him close to where I was living. He was in the family room meditating. Then, suddenly, he came into the dining room, and as I see him, he just says two words: **TWO FORCES!** He got it, a two primary forces, equal and opposite. Now that is balance! Let's recall Robert's e-mail letter* to me: *"In your writings, you have defined the TRUE nature of the WORD as being PROCREATIVE and the ONE order, context, process, and structure of the universe and that MAN and WOMAN are its TWO electrodes of manifesting!"* That is different from his statement, *"I am this moment,"* which he would state from time to time. Robert was into meditation. He would go deep into the stillness, a stillness located at a placement deeper than the mind. But it became a "two force" balance/stillness. The still point is actually Unity. In that moment, deep into the balance/stillness, Robert made the shift—**TWO FORCES!** *"We together are this moment!"*

*His e-mail letter came to me sometime after his visit.

There are two primary forces in creation. One is male; the other is female. See how they work together, dividing apart and uniting together. There cannot be a singular "God." There cannot be a Virgin Birth nor a Jesus as the one and only "Son of God." Where is the **Daughter of God**? There cannot even be a singular Stillness/Unity. The balance of life only exists in a Man and a Woman <u>creating life together</u>. Recall this earlier quote followed by a quote from *The Two Forces of Creation.*

...and the TWO shall become as ONE—Encoded in the Book of Eternal Life © 2010; Meditations for Deepening Love © 1994

In the heart of every man and woman, the TWO, is placed the eternal desire to become as ONE. This desire is known as love. "May I give my life to you," the man shouts. "Yes, please do," the woman responds. And out of this love a new birth of life, a new born boy or girl, is brought forth as the eternal desire moves on. The ONE has just become the TWO again. This eternal process is called the *procreant*—a procreative process of balanced interchange between the TWO and the ONE.

And so the TWO becomes as ONE. Not a ONE of no TWO, but a TWO within a ONE for, procreantly, every ONE will again become a TWO. Within the ONE is always the divided TWO. Within the TWO is always the united ONE.

The Two Forces of Creation © 1988—Selected Writings, Volume 2 © 1991, 2010

In review, let me suggest that "what is," is relationship-in-process. Relationship-in-process is fundamental or primordial, not a First Cause or One Force. This is to further say that there isn't a supreme being although there may be supreme beings. There isn't a mover of the spheres although there may be movers of the spheres. There isn't a one God who sees all that becomes or forms all immortal beings although there may be gods that do just that.* There is not a single fundamental primordial creative force in the universe, i.e., energy, desire, motive, impulse, purpose, impetus, drive, intention, nature, will, consciousness. Prana, mana, Ki. Chi, Waken, bioplasma, light, cosmic energy, life force, vital pulse, or Holy Spirit. There is only one force in relationship to another force from which creation may then occur. We have to date made a critical mistake in not noting this elementary fact within our conception of order.

*Some language taken from the early Greek philosopher Pythagoras, 570-500 B.C.

"There is not a single fundamental primordial creative force in the universe…" This was and is one of the fundamental insights given to me in my early 30s from which this whole development of the conception of Man and Woman Balance, i.e., a New Trinity rests. Here is another one. *"There is only one force in relationship to another force from which creation may then occur."*

This is the Trinity for the **(Pro)Creation of Life**. The life process is Man, Woman, and Son or Daughter. Christianity did not make this procreant distinction. It became about "My Eternal Life" first and You second.

H. Spencer Lewis—*The Secret Doctrine of Jesus*, 1937

"The Christian religion—the Christian form of churchianity—is one of the most complex systems of today, as compared with the extreme and magnificent simplicity of the system unfolded by Jesus."

Rev. G. Maurice Elliot—*The Psychic Life of Jesus*, 1938

"When the Church is 'established' the 'signs and wonders' cease to be performed.

"What is this truth all about?

"Harnack, Principal Cairns, and Dr, Glover have given us the facts.

"Harnack writes: 'The Church now had its priests, its altars, its sacraments, and its Holy Book...But it no longer possessed the spirit and the power of the spirit.'

"Principal Cairns writes: 'The miracles of the spirit gradually ceased, because by compromise with the world the Church got out of touch with the pure grace of God. It no longer possessed the strong, unconventional faith of the first generation.'

"Dr. Glover writes: 'The ministry of the spirit, the ministry of 'gifts' was succeeded by the ministry of Office with its lower ideals of the practical and the expedient.'

"That was it! That is it!

"Miracles ceased when the Church became unworthy of them.

"Miracles are unclassified phenomena. They are not unnatural. They are not supernatural. They are supernormal. Yesterday's miracles are today's natural laws. The most natural laws are spiritual laws, for Man is spirit.

"Jesus came to reveal God to Man, and Man to himself.

"Jesus taught men that they could be as he, and do the works that he did, if only they would *think* as he thought, *trust* as he trusted, *pray* as he prayed.

"The church in ascribing the miracles of Jesus to his Godhead has made a fatal mistake. She has divorced Jesus from the rest of Humanity."

"She has divorced Jesus from the rest of Humanity." Indeed. The Christian religion today is no more than churchianity. Jesus' message, if I may suggest, was no more than *Love ye one another*. And that is as spiritual as things get. So how can we do that? It is simple; be in the balance. Don't say, "I Am," but rather say **"I Am and You Are."** And we can add to that, **"We Together Are."** We do not exist singularly but in tandem. We cannot have Man without Woman or Woman without Man. Remember the verse **Genesis**

1:27: *So God created man in his own image, in the image of God created he him, male and female created he them.* If God created *male and female created he them* so then must not "God" be of this one creative order of two forces? Think of "God" as the point of unification and Male and Female as the points of division.

Christianity is in collapse today due to the failure of mankind to make the sexual/procreation distinction on the spiritual level. Has the church stood up to the global money changers that have fostered counterfeit (debt) money—and economic slavery—upon us all? Or how about the WHO and big Pharma wanting to dictate/control our health decisions, i.e., vaccines (poisons) for everyone. (How many vaccines are now being recommended for children in the first two years of their lives?) *"But don't we get to have a choice?" "Oh no. It is for your own good; I can assure you." "But don't we get to know what is in these shots?" "Oh no. You must follow our guidance and take them. It is for your own good you know." "But what if there are side effects? Will I be compensated if there are negative side effects to my health?" "Of course not; we have absolute immunity from lawsuits."*

Or how about the Woke* mentality of "the only absolute is that there are no absolutes." Isn't metaphysical relativity the door the LGBTPQ folks are walking through, demanding it is their way or no way? I recently heard that the Pope came out in favor of giving a blessing to LGBTPQ couples. Is this to give a blessing to sodomy? Or to "marriages" of threesomes or eightsomes? Or for aborting babies even up to the time of birth? Or for "sex change" operations for children? Or for sex-trafficking of children? Or even to pedophiles? They should get a blessing, right? How about a blessing for those who use adrenochrome—Corporate bigwigs, political elites, Hollywood movie stars, etc. or anyone? It seems to me that things are backwards; that some or many would rather make it a "crime" to misgender another? Perhaps even a "hate crime" for those who insist on believing in man, woman, and child? Imagine that. We just don't get it? We are crippled! We are done! Gender dysphoria is upon us. Spiritually speaking, we are out of balance with one another. We have become lost souls and do not know what to do.

*It appears to me that the "Woke movement" is but another name for the various forms fascism takes—do or else. Could I be wrong in my analysis? Perhaps. But just go to a LGBTQ pride parade. What do you see? I believe we should be having Man, Woman, and Child parades!

Elizabeth Bellhouse— Measureless Healing

"In one glance I saw all Nature as she is: crippled, bewildered, and crying out for aid. I heard her manyfold pitiful cries and saw the ubiquity of her pitiful state—and I experienced her despairing agony….

"What that Experience conveyed to me was that man requires healing so fundamental: at a depth so great, that he is re-enabled to align himself with God's concept of him… God made man in his own image with (therefore God-like) power over all creation, *(Gen. 1:26) and put him in the Garden of Eden to dress it and keep it." (Gen. 2:15)*

"*…that man requires healing so fundamental: at a depth so great, that he is **re-enabled to align himself with God's concept of him.**" Do you hear these words? Our pain/hurt is so deep that we cannot get out from under it. Let's continue with Elizabeth Bellhouse.

Elizabeth Bellhouse—*Measureless Healing*

"Not only blessings, for this was a period filled with, above all, perceptions (intimations) of the nature of Purity. It seemed God wanted me to become as fully aware of the inescapability of Purity as He had wanted me to be vividly aware of the quality of The Beginning. I was confronted with the necessity of overcoming spiritual fault rather than psychological wrong.

" …Not that the Old Testament itself denies the feminine aspect of God—SHE was simply not acceptable to the people for who it was written and so was not taken up any more than God as de facto king could be kept up. Christ did not deny the feminine aspect of God.

"Since, in this book, we are searching for the Whole, and since in the Whole femininity and masculinity are co-mingled and of the amalgam of the two the Whole's form is made: since we are searching for the perfect balance of outlook and vision: for as near total comprehension as we can achieve, we have to look into this also.

"A little while back we saw that what is needed is that oneself and all one's parts (one's body and soul) and their parts and functions become more nearly one with God in essence and quality. It is, therefore, essential to take an objective look at what we have turned our backs on: the feminine aspect of the androgynous God on who the human being is modeled. That in whose image we were created male and female."

"…we have turned our backs on: the feminine aspect of the androgynous God on who the human being is modeled." Do you get it? Even to this day, the female force has not been considered as equally necessary as the male force. (And don't for one minute think that the LBGTPQ movement is somehow on the side of female.) The female desire/force is the Unity of the Two. The male desire/force is the Division of the One. May I suggest that the "One" is not comprised of an "androgynous God," as if the Unity of the Two somehow comprises a bisexual nor non-sexual essence, or as if the "One" is somehow outside of or prior to the two-force procreant life process. The procreant life process is comprised to two equal and opposite forces, male and female. These two forces unite together and divide apart. There is a balance incorporated in their interaction together. If that balance is lost so, too, is their love together, their purity of heart, and their children. Historically, it has been a Man's world. Women, in their quest for equality, bought into Feminism (equal but not opposite). This, unfortunately, opened the door to sexual relativity, i.e., LGBTPQ etc. In result, the woman is hurt once more. Her soul is injured. Her womb is empty. Where is her equal and opposite other half? She, woman, is alone, to face the "Nothingness" by herself alone. And the men laugh once more.

This, my friends, is the hurt, the emptiness, the void. And men, those of you who are here only to take from women, or claim you are "gay" or even "trans," you do not get off so easy. You are denying life itself. Your purpose is to lead; fatherly love leads all things. A woman's purpose is to love. Motherly love heals all things.

I mean, let us just ask, why the two sexes/two parent family unit to begin with?

Genesis 1:27: *So God created man in his own image, in the image of God created he him, male and female created he them.*

Genesis 1:28: *And God blessed them, and God said unto them, Be fruitful, and multiply, and replenish the earth, and subdue it: and have dominion over the fish of the sea, and over the fowl of the air, and over every living thing that moveth upon the earth.*

Genesis 2:24: *Therefore shall a man leave his father and his mother, and shall cleave unto his wife: and they shall be one flesh.*

Genesis 6:19: *And of every living thing of all flesh, two of every sort shalt thou bring into the ark, to keep them alive with thee; they shall be male and female.*

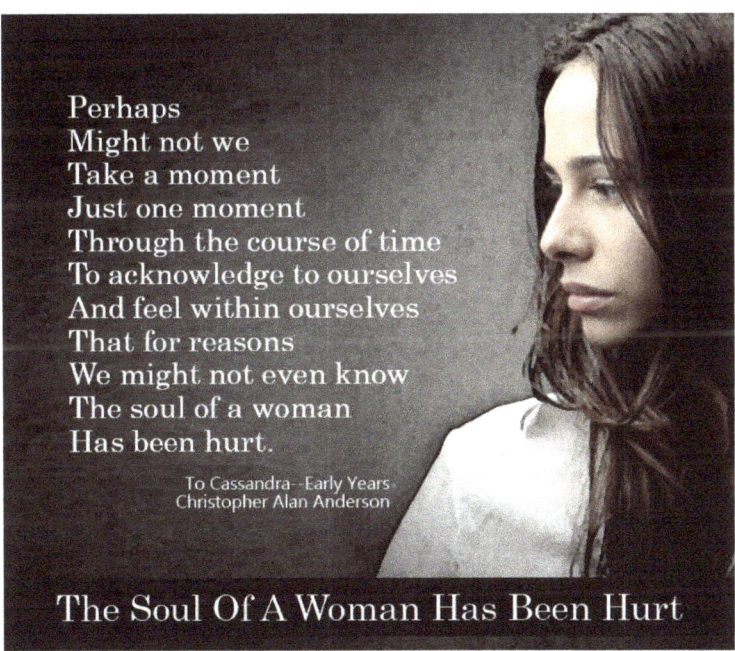

Our savior, as it were, lies in our ***sexual balance together***. Salvation comes in pairs, not singularity. This is what the **New Trinity** brings to us. It is comprised of an equal and opposite balance, **God the Father, God the Mother, and God the Holy Son**

or Holy Daughter. If you still want to use the term *Christ* think in terms of Christ (male) and Christa (female). There cannot be an unsexed or unisex Christ. There cannot be a Virgin Birth Christ. We must correct the Trintiy to align to the procreant process of all life. ***The New Trintiy has procreation incorporated into it at the spiritual level.*** We got close in Christianity. Unfortunately, we were left with the "Trinity" of God the Father, the Mother of Jesus, and Jesus as the Only begotten Son. We have "God," the Holy Mother, and the Christ Jesus. Where is Jesus' wife to be found, and their children? Oh, but we cannot allow Jesus to be a sexual man with sexual desire for a woman. No, Jesus must be our savior; he can't have a wife and they together have children. He must be our savior, "I" demand it! After all, our own "Eternal Life" comes first, right? We are stuck in an imbalance at the spiritual level of life. And we cannot get out unless or until we balance our own metaphysics in our hearts/souls. The **New Trinity** presents to us this sexual/procreant balance from where we may now state:

> ***If there is a God the Father there must also be a God the Mother, not a God the Mother as a secondary existence to God the Father but as an equal and opposite primary existence to God the Father.***

Under the New Trintiy we would not allow a blessing be given to "homosexual couples" or any LGBTPQ misalignment. LGBTPQ does not incorporate the Procreant Life process into its center point. Instead, we have the glorification of sodomy, transsexualism, pedophilia, and even child sex trafficking and sacrifice. How is that to work? The New Trinity gives to us **Rebirth**. It is our **resurrection** into Procreative (Life) Balance. It is this **New Trinity** that will heal our hearts and purify our souls. Nothing else will do.

Sigmund Freud (1856-1939)—*The Sexual Life of Human Beings*
"The abandonment of the reproductive function is the common feature of all perversions. We actually describe a sexual activity as perverse if it has given up the aim of reproduction and pursues the attainment of pleasure as an aim independent of it. So, as you will see, the reach and turning point in the development of sexual life lies in becoming subordinate to the purpose of reproduction. Everything that happens before this turn of events and equally everything that disregards it and that aims solely at obtaining pleasure is given the uncomplimentary name of "perverse" and as such is proscribed."

"We actually describe a sexual activity as perverse if it has given up the aim of reproduction and pursues the attainment of pleasure as an aim independent of it." Do you get it?— *"…as an aim independent of it."* Sound familiar in today's culture of Gender Queer Identity—fluid and changing.

Let's again review verse from the Bible. What more need be said?

Genesis 6:19: *And of every living thing of all flesh, two of every sort shalt thou bring into the ark, to keep them alive with thee; they shall be male and female.*

…they shall they be male and female? But why? Isn't that self-evident—it is for **Procreation,** the continuity of **Life**!

Then there is a quote from one of my writings.

The 2008-2009 Articles—Homosexuality is not a Sexuality © 2010
Homosexuality is not a sexuality. Wow, what kind of statement is that? Certainly, that can't be tolerant of other's choices and

commitments, can it? In fact, if one were to utter such a thing, we might think that one is some fundamentalist type ideologue who rants and raves against homosexuality. Perhaps a little "re-education" is called for to "enlighten" that person to today's progressive and tolerant ways. At the least we should find a way to silence that one—outlawing such "hate" speech or writings or whatever the vehicle of expression might be. We need to be sure we don't actually inquire into what that statement—*homosexuality is not a sexuality*—might really mean. We don't want to take the chance that it might have some merit to it. Maybe that would expose the deepest illusions of our own souls. No, better to cut this off as soon as possible. But I do kind of wonder, what does that statement mean?

Sexuality/Gender is not a relative term. It is not a Social Construct. It is not decided by one's current whim. It is absolute/concrete. **Two Forces!** It lies in Man and Woman Balance—**Equal and Opposite**. If sexuality/family can be anything, any mixing or pairing or activity one decides on any given day, then it is means nothing. LGBTPQ is nothing more than the completion of the Marxist dream of the abolition of the family (Man, Woman, and Child) unit of procreation, of LIFE. In short, LGBTPQ is the **denial of life**. And it will, absolutely, destroy anything that it touches, and that includes Christianity. Look at what is happening to the Christian church today. It is splintering apart. There is no going back. But beware, if you dare believe in the two-parent family metaphysically (Man and Woman as the fundamental life process), you just may find yourself charged with hate crime and perhaps even jailed. Let that sink in.

Having said this, let me be clear, I am not in any way advocating violence (any use of force) against one who may believe they are homosexual or of any LGBTPQ type, or against any believer in a religion or political persuasion. I am simply suggesting that if there is to be any type of healing for our souls it will only come through love. The New Trintiy is the Trintiy of Love.

John 4:24: *God is a Spirit: and they that worship him must worship him in spirit and in truth.*

John 15:12: *This is my commandment, that ye love one another, as I have loved you.*

The New Trinity is also a **Trinity of Metaphysical Law**. Life is sustained by our aligning to Metaphysical Law/Balance—to the Two Equal and Opposite Forces of Life. So let us not advocate violence but, at the same time, let us stand up for Law—*and for our families*. Love (Female) and Law (Male); that is the Life Balance.

Aristotle's Laws of Logic Pertaining to Sexuality

The Law of Identity – Male is male; Female is female.

The Law of Non-Contradiction – Male is not Female; Female is not Male.

The Law of the Excluded Middle – Everything is either Male or Female. (What is not Male is Female; what is not Female is Male.)

The Law of Connection – Male is not without Female; Female is not without Male.

Healing In The Light: Male and Female Division and Unification © 1998

-Does every man have a woman and every woman a man?

Yes, from the beginning. From the unity we divide into our sexual parts. From division we unite. It is a procreative, sexual process. The male purpose is to divide the one and secure sexual form. The female purpose is to unite the two and reproduce sexual form. Without both the male function and the female function, in balance, we just aren't able to make it.

-So each of us has an opposite?

Yes. We don't come alone. I call this opposite one's other half or eternal companion.

The 2008-2009 Articles—Love: The Law of Polar Opposites © 2010

Only (sexual) opposites can unite to then again divide...creating the spiritual lineage of (procreant) love.

The Two Forces of Creation © 1988, Selected Writings: Volume 2 © 1991

The two faces of love are reflected in a male and a female. Each of these faces is different from the other, yet they each convey one of the two aspects of love. The two aspects of love are male individualization and female unification in interaction together. Love is male and female in rhythmic balanced interchange.

The face of a man reveals his stand, holding the division of male and female secure in creation. A man's face reflects the depth of his stand and shows his capacity to love. The face of a woman reveals her stand, holding the unity of male-female within herself from which the next division of creation will occur. A woman's face also reflects the depth of her stand in showing her capacity to love. The depth of their love together will be dependent on the knowledge they hold of their sexual essence from which they then act. The key to love and the capacity to surrender lies in the two distinct sexual essences of male and female and our knowledge (consciousness) of that.

The Discovery of Life © 1994

A man and a woman, in the universe, meet and recognize each other as the one that they have known throughout all time. They know, for they each have taken the leap into their own sexual universality and can say *I am not alone*. They stand together on the foundation of life forevermore knowing:

Who am "I"?

"I" am a male in relationship to a female,
or
"I" am a female in relationship to a male

. . . whichever sexuality "I" happen to be,

"You" being the sexual opposite of me.

And they look into each other's eyes knowing for all time:

Why am "I" here?

"I" am here to express the sexuality that "I" am . . .

-Male, being that force which seeks to individualize a

form separate and apart from the unity of male-female.

-Female, being that force which seeks to unite separate

forms together from the division of male and female.

. . . so that together we may continue to manifest our

own sexual creation.

A man and a woman meet and a miracle occurs—a new life is formed. The miracle of life is held within their balance and love. Life, all of life, is held within their balance and love.

The Man and Woman Relationship

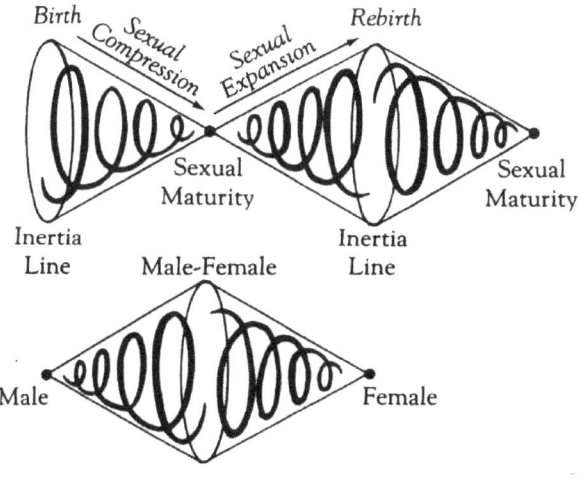

There is just no getting around the **Two Procreant Forces of Creation**. The **Two Procreant Forces of Creation** is our absolute, i.e., the **Metaphysical Given** of our lives. Try as you may, the **Metaphysical Given of Life** cannot be ignored. Christianity, or any religion; Socialism, or any form of political fascism; and Homosexuality, or any variation of LGBTPQ, cannot take us to the promised land of **Procreant Love**. Procreant Love is our absolute, the only absolute based in <u>Life</u> itself. It's <u>Procreant Love</u> or it's Nothingness. Which do you pick? The New Trinity, comprised of Man and Woman Balance, is our healing and our salvation. It opens the door to Procreant Love. Procreant Love is the basis of Spiritual Healing. Actually, it is the basis of all of <u>Life</u>. Procreant Love places us in Universal Alignment with our equal and opposite other half which is the balance point of all things. Spiritual healing is but a balance of being, one to another. It is based in the New Trinity. The New Trinity comprises the balance that is Man and Woman Balance, the only balance there is.

"…the only balance there is." Is this something we can integrate within ourselves, something we can base our lives upon, something we can stand face to face with another (man to woman and woman to man) and state: "I am here for you; I give my life to you"?

Elizabeth Barrett Browning (1806-1861)

"I love you not only for what you are,

but for what I am when I am with you.

I love you not only for what you have made of yourself,

but for what you are making of me.

I love you for the part of me that you bring out."

The Holy Spirit Has Come

*"...that man requires healing so fundamental: at a depth so great, that he is **re-enabled to align himself with God's concept of him.**"*

"...we have turned our backs on: the feminine aspect of the androgynous God on who the human being is modeled."

Did you hear these words from Elizabeth Bellhouse? Our pain/hurt is so deep that we cannot get out from under it. Moreover, we don't know what to do. Right now, a good portion of the world is clamoring for war! The Deep State oligarchs and political elites running the counterfeit money cabal can't hardly wait. It is all about power and money. Not just woman, but men, and boys, have taken it on the chops as well. These endless (Deep State) wars, taking young men to their slaughter. No, not those who orchestrate these wars, not those who make money off these wars, not those who call the shots in the backrooms while smoking their cigars, no; it's the men ordered to rush the line, or beach, that take the hit/death, a couple thousand here, a few million there, as long as we, the Deep Staters, retain power and make money. And so it is….thousands, and even millions, of lives lost. We need to turn this all around. We need to get control of our government's world over. Leaders, even if elected, are not holier than thou. They, too, must abide by the same rules we must abide by. Political monarchies days are over. Balance/Sovereigncy (a Constitutional Republic) has come to stay. Leaders, too, must abide by the same rules/laws they make us, We the People, abide by. No more perks, pensions, medical plans, secret investments, kickbacks, etc. that We the People do not have access to. No more handing out OUR money to special causes for special favors. No more hiding behind "laws" so you don't have to come clean with We the People. No more special appointments for bureaucrats who hide under the claim of immunity or Judges who claim to be outside of or above the law. No more Washington D.C. Inc. control of states, only sovereign states controlled by the people. No more assigning our Sovereigncy over to world organizations such as the WHO or World Bank or UN….not to mention the FED and IRS. Do you want the truth, i.e., the Metaphysical Truth I mean? You, and I, must want the TRUTH, all the way down to our souls. The Truth cometh to them that ask. Okay, no more killing of babies. No more LGBTPQ curriculum in schools. Family first then Community, State, and Federal. Marriage limited to one man and one woman as is the **Universal Order of Life**.

The Legend of the Truth © 1991; Meditations for Deepening Love © 1995, 2010

…Behold, my friends, you have sought for the truth within you. But you findeth it not. We have come to say unto you—the whole of the truth lieth not in your hearts alone. No, rather, one half of the truth lieth in man and the other half of the truth lieth in woman. You can only find this truth together. The whole of the truth lieth in the hearts of man and woman and is only revealed when a man and a woman cometh together in their love.

Let Us Create Life Together © 1991; Meditations for Deepening Love © 1995, 2010

The woman was beginning to see the magnitude of the man's responses. The truth cannot be spoken—she had no idea. "But," the woman spoke, "how do you hold all of this within yourself over time? It must break your heart." The woman looked at the man and suddenly begins to flush. She saw that this man did carry a broken heart—so within himself he seemed to be. "What can I do to help?" she uttered. "We don't want the truth to die." The man responded saying, "The truth lives only as it is *reproduced.* The truth lives only through man and woman. If I have been sent with this message then I must not have been sent alone." The man paused and then trembled as he said, *"May you be the one who has been sent with me. May you be the one to extend beyond me."*

John 4:24: *God is a Spirit: and they that worship him must worship him in spirit and in truth.*

"But where is this Spirit?" Might I also ask, "What or who is this Spirit?" Perhaps these verses will shed some light.

John 12:35-36: *Yet a little while is the light with you. Walk while ye have the light, lest darkness come upon you: for he that walketh in darkness knoweth not whither he goeth. While ye have light, believe in the light, that ye may be the children of light.*

John 14:17: *Even the Spirit of truth; whom the world cannot receive, because it seeth him not, neither knoweth him: but ye know him: for he dwelleth with you, and shall be in you.*

John 14:18: *I will not leave you comfortless: I will come to you.*

John 14:26: *But the Comforter, which is the Holy Ghost, whom the Father will send in my name, he shall teach you all things, and bring all things to your remembrance, whatsoever I have said unto you.*

John 16: 7-8: *Nevertheless I tell you the truth; It is expedient for you that I go away: for if I go not away, the Comforter will not come unto you; but if I depart, I will send him unto you. And when he is come, he will reprove the world of sin, and of righteousness, and of judgment.*

John 16:12: *I have yet many things to say unto you, but ye cannot bear them now.*

John 16:13: *Howbeit when he, the Spirit of truth, is come, he will guide you into all truth: for he shall not speak of himself; but whatsoever he shall hear, that shall he speak: and he will shew you things to come.*

John 16:22: *And ye now therefore have sorrow: but I will see you again, and your heart shall rejoice, and your joy no man taketh from you.*

"But the Comforter, which is the Holy Ghost, whom the Father will send in my name…." May I now suggest, the Comforter, which is the Holy Ghost (who I refer to as the **Holy Spirit**) has already been sent to us. He, or she, already resides amongst us.

William Stainton Moses (1839-1892) —Spirit Teachings
"It is the spiritual return. There will be no such physical return as man has dreamed of. This will be the return to his people, by the voice of His Messengers speaking to those whose ears are open; even as He himself said. 'He that hath ears to hear, let him hear; he that is able to receive it, let him receive it.' Is this message coming to many? Yes, to many it is being made known that God is now specially influencing man at this epoch. We man no say more. May the blessing of the Supreme rest on you."

The Holy Spirit has come. Actually, the Holy Spirit has never left. The Holy Spirit lives in us now. Can you feel her calling you now? I say her because the Holy Spirit is the **Spirit of Woman**. She, woman, is the Spirit of Unity, of Unconditional Love. Men, don't look to Jesus for your salvation, look to a woman. And women, look to a man, a man who knows and honors the **Spirit of Woman**.

Yes, it is the **Spirit of Woman** who is the **Holy Spirit**, also called the **Eternal Woman**. You think I jest? Who else can the Holy Spirit be than the **Unitive Spirit of Woman**—the Woman who has been cast aside and thrown away—and yet still embraces all with her unitive love?

Channeling the Eternal Woman © 2014
The Eternal Woman is true Source. Now notice, always within the Eternal Woman is Individual Man. Individual Man is the counter-balance of the Eternal Woman. The Eternal Woman is the death-rebirth point of all life. (The Individual Man is the birth-life point of all life.) She is the field, the space, the opening, the connection, the intuition, the universal, the feeling, the relation, the continuity, and the home—and her force is equal in strength to Individual Man although opposite in function.

The Eternal Woman is the soul of each and every woman. I believe that every woman knows this. And yet, it seems that many women are cut off from the Eternal Woman within them. They perhaps have forgotten that they are the universal connective point between all things. Men, too, have apparently forgotten this. If men really understood the essence of a woman, they would treat women as Gods. The only thing a woman wants is to be loved. Is that so wrong? A man wants to be believed in. That is his glory.

Thank you. I am the Eternal Woman. I am not a "God." I am a woman. I am the female soul within every woman. As a woman, I stand with man. Actually, I stand between man and child. I am the link between man and child. I am the space between man and child. I am the death of all life and the life of all death. From a man dying inside of me, so our child is born out of me. I am what you might call the field, frame, zero-point, space, opening, womb, or void. But I am not death. Rather, I give life to death. I bring life-potential to all things. I connect all things within me. In this, I am love. Without me there would never be love. All women know this about me because they know it about themselves.

I want you to know that I, the Eternal Woman, answer each and every prayer request made to me. Actually, all prayers are to me. As I have said, I am the space or field. Some call me the eternal void. But I am not empty space or a field without miracles. I am the tomb that all individual things die into and I am the womb that gives rebirth to all individual things. Know me as fertility. I will give rebirth to whatever you give to me. I am perfect balance. Each and every prayer that you asketh of me, I replay back to you as to your intent. Did you hear me? I give back to you in equal measure as per your intention. Could I do otherwise?

Can you feel her pain which is also her *love*? (The Soul of a Woman has been hurt.) To heal this hurt, we, men and women, must recognize our eternal balance *together*. Why together? Don't men first need to ask for forgiveness? Perhaps, but let us remember men have been hurt as well. These endless wars, young men going to their slaughter. Who is directing this? We must stand together and say *"No more."*

P.P. Quimby (1802-1866)—*The Quimby Manuscripts* © **1921**
"...that all diseases of the body are caused by a derangement of the mind! And that the cure of all diseases may be affected, theoretically, by a restoration or rectification of the mind of the invalid, to its natural, proper condition. He has this faith, and when he succeeds in imparting it to the patient, the disease vanishes and the whole person is restored to harmonious natural functions. His formula of faith is confessedly that of the Saviour and the woman who touched the hem of his garment and became whole. The operation is purely mental. Mr. Q. discards this scriptural fact as a "miracle," but regards it as natural, as properly reproductive by those who have the right idea of diseases and their cure, and who have the faith to attempt to relieve human suffering."

"...that all diseases of the body are caused by a derangement of the mind!" Might we just say that all diseases are caused, or are equal to, the imbalance one carries within one's soul?

Mark 5:30, 34: *...Who touched my clothes? ...Daughter, thy faith hath made thee whole; go in peace, and be whole of thy plague.*

"*...Daughter, thy faith hath made thee whole....*" Why faith? What exactly is faith? Might it be the balance point of sexual/procreant, i.e., an alignment between a man and a woman. Let's let the **Divine Masculine** and the **Divine Feminine** touch together in their fundament need for each other. This, the **procreant touch** is that fundament somethingness that allows us to shine the spiritual light unto each other that takes us out of the Black Hole of Nothingness, a nothingness that permeates all religious, political, and sexual imbalances. **Let us live together for only together can we live.**

The Return of the Holy Spirit lies in the acknowledgement of the Soul of Woman, a Soul equal to but opposite from the Soul of Man. Woman is the **Holy Spirit**. She is the **Divine Feminine**, the **God the Mother**. She embraces the **Procreant Touch** which is **Eternal Life** itself. We men need to acknowledge this Truth. Then, from that point, we can also say that the Holy Spirit lives in the **Balance of Man and Woman**. Afterall, it takes a Man and a Woman to make a baby!

To Cassandra—Early Years © 1985, 1994

Touch

At times
At times in this universe
We come upon each other
And touch
Briefly,
Or for a longer spell
Lightly,
Or only we can tell,
We touch
Male and female
Each touch
Securing and reproducing
A complete touch,
And all we really know
Is the love
Between ourselves
And our other half.
Man and woman
Live
And struggle
And walk and rest
And die and concentrate
And hope and exaggerate
And despair and recreate
Only, only

Always together.
Cassandra,
Shall you and I
Walk into our silence
Together
Down the aisle
Arm and arm
Into the abyss
Forever
Only to return
When called by desire
Between a man and a woman
To touch.

When called by desire between a man and a woman to touch. Men, the Holy Spirit is waiting to be touched, not just physically, not even mentally/intellectually, but in SPIRIT.

Our Eternal Life Together

The eternal is that which is ***procreative to life.*** And how does this ***Spirit of Eternal Life*** come to us? Through the ***Holy Spirit***. The Holy Spirit brings to us <u>Purity</u> and <u>Grace</u>. Purity presents to us a pure/clean soul. Grace presents to us Metaphysical Balance, i.e. **LOVE.** Grace actually is **Spiritual Perfection.** It is a state of balance between two souls.—**a TOUCH.** Many if not most of us are tied into an imbalanced belief system. We cannot get out for we do not know we are locked into it much less know where to even go. Shall we "meditate in the stillness." Maybe we can "study philosophy." (Not that I am against meditation or study of metaphysical Principle and Process.) Or even better how about a study of "the mind" with all its psychological "I know best" propaganda attached. And if none of that works we can always fall back on religion. Actually, I do find a number of verses in the Bible to be of merit. Here are a few.

Matthew 5:8: *Blessed are the pure in heart: for they shall see God.*

Matthew 5:16: *Let your light so shine before men, that they may see your good works, and glorify your Father, which is in heaven.*

Matthew 5:44: *But I say unto you, Love your enemies, bless them that curse you, do good to them that hate you, and pray for them which despitefully use you, and persecute you.*

Matthew 5:48: *Be ye therefore perfect, even as your Father which is in heaven is perfect.*

And yet, we still seem to not be able to get to Spirit (the ***Spirit of Eternal Life , i.e.,*** the ***Holy Spirit)***.

The following is a quote made on Facebook by Giselle Walker. I met Giselle in the Senior Assisted Living complex we both have been staying at. She has helped me get back on my feet again. We have become very close, two souls united. She, too, has made the distinction of ***two forces***. She is responding to a Facebook acquaintance regarding an artist's perception.

"The artist's endeavor in any medium is to 'speak' in such a manner so as to evoke an emotional response from their invited guest. The hope is to touch another's soul, this the most basic of mankind's needs, clearly being that which utterly defines us. Through having touched another, we have lent proof to our very existence, thus allowing us to touch the face of Eternity."

"Through having touched another, we have lent proof to our very existence, thus allowing us to touch the face of Eternity." Not to different from **Mark 5:30, 34:** *...Who touched my clothes? ...Daughter, thy faith hath made thee whole; go in peace, and be whole of thy plague.*) Whether we touch another or are touched by another, this is the healing, the New Trinity, our Universal Balance, our Spiritual Resurrection which is our Eternal Life together. **We can go no further then touching another or being touched by another—they go hand-in-hand.**

Now, let us take a moment and turn to science. I often hear the claim, "Well, this can't be science." or "You haven't any proof." I wonder, can feeling the emotion of love within oneself, by one giving love to or receiving love from another, that can't be science?

Henry David Thoreau (1817 – 1862)
"With all your science, can you tell me how it is that light comes into the soul?"

Might I suggest that Mr. Thoreau is speaking of a ***spiritual light***. A light behind the mind as it were. And this spiritual light brings love to each one of us for this spiritual light is really but our ***procreant balance together***. And it has now come to each one of us who knows of the New Trintiy, the Trinity of Man and Woman Balance. ***And a child is born!***

I wonder, has science ever brought to us the pure heart? What seems to be on the horizon with science is AI and biological or genetic altering of our very essences. Is this what we want? Our **Eternal Life Together** is not about either. Life is a procreant life process between the two equal and opposite forces of male and female, i.e., Birth-Life-Death-Rebirth. Death is but a resting point. It is the exhalation that comes with inhalation, the rest that comes with effort, the expansion that comes with compression, etc. There is an immorality of spirit—it is the exact **Life Process of Man and Woman Balance**. Such is the First Principle and the Upholding Principle. (See quote below.) It is the Procreant Life Process itself.

Elizabeth Bellhouse—*Measureless Healing*
"If we are to live in God and God in us, then we must become as aware as we can be of the nature of that in which we live and move and have our being. That which indwells us, permeates all our being, and surrounds us before and behind, to the right, and to the left, and is above us, and beneath us. That which is *both the First Principle and the Upholding Principle of the whole scheme of Creation.*

" *'Make your home in Me',* he said continuing the same theme, *'as I make mine in you. If you remain in me and my words remain in you, you may ask what you will and you shall get it. Believe the works for they prove the Father is in me and that I am in Him. The Father has given Me power over all flesh.'"*

"Make your home in Me as I make mine in you." Is not this the TOUCH? Prayer, what we might call true prayer or answered prayer, is nothing more than a TOUCH, one unto another. What we call the Son of God is but a TOUCH, one unto another. The term Christ, as in Jesus Christ or Jesus the Christ is simply a TOUCH, one unto another. You, when you touch another or are touched by another, TOUCH the very Heart of God—both Father <u>and</u> Mother. The TOUCH, if you will, is our salvation/resurrection. *"If Christ be raised our faith is true; we are in love together."* Let's state it this way: *"When we touch together our lives are made true; we are in a state of GRACE together."*

Christian D. Larson (1874-1954)—*The Ideal Made Real*
"The prayer that is uttered through the spirit of faith and through the soul of thanksgiving—the two united in one, is always answered, whether it be uttered silently or audibly."

William Stainton Moses (1839-1892)—*Spirit Teachings*

"True prayer is the ready voice of spirit communing with spirit: the cry of the soul to invisible friends with whom it is used to speak: the flashing along the magnetic line a message of request which brings, swift as thought, its ready answer back."

The New Trinity is but a TOUCH. How could it be anything more? Again, the word CHRIST actually means *touch*. Jesus touched another and in that touch there was a spiritual realignment and thus healing. Jesus in touching another was also touched by another. **Mark 5:30, 34:** *…Who touched my clothes? …Daughter, thy faith hath made thee whole; go in peace, and be whole of thy plague.*) We have turned Jesus into a one-way street. Yet, he needed the **Touch** as much as anyone. Our giving and receiving of love *one to another* is the touch, and in this touch is our own spiritual realignment and our healing—for all time. One unto another. Man to woman and woman to man. We together comprise the Touch of Christ.

John 10:30: *I and my Father are one.*

My legal scholar friend, Ron MacDonald, who helped my Father and me through our 6 years of IRS hell, said one word to me after I had been explaining to him the equal and opposite metaphysics of Man and Woman Balance. That one word was **EQUIPOISE**! Equipoise—Counter Balance—Equal and Opposite. Equipoise equals Touch. The Touch is the New Trintiy. **The Touch is Life**. There isn't anything in Life but Life. And all Life is Eternal Life. And our *Eternal Life* begins right now—***We together are this moment.***

THE

DIVINE TOUCH

A NEW CREATION FOR LIFE

"I see a light no man or woman has ever seen. The unseen world is now the seen and known world; its order is beautiful, its balance perfect. Yes, I see a new world, the most Divine world that has ever come to pass. And I can even <u>prove</u> it to you, for, you see, I now see You."

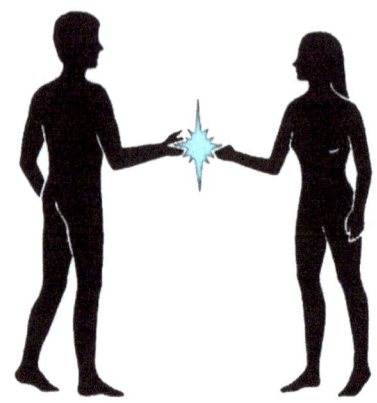

The Divine Touch: A New Creation for Life © 2021

Our touch together is our spiritual healing. It lies in the New Trintiy of God the Father, God the Mother, and God the Holy Son and/or Holy Daughter. It lies in the New Trinity of Marriage. Marriage is a Holy Touch between one Man and one Woman. Our purpose as man and woman pairs is to touch in love and, in so doing, *create life together.* Let this be our stand!

**Only marriage between one man and one woman
is valid or recognized in the Universe!**

The 2008-2009 Articles - I Will Life Up Mine Eyes © 2010

Can we now define love? Might we begin with the terms Father and Mother? Or how about Husband and Wife? *Procreant balance*—(the Omnific term)—and a child, son or daughter, is born. *Spiritual procreation*—(the Omnific term)--operating everywhere at all times, reflecting back to us the love that resides in our hearts. Two forces, male and female, equal and opposite, dividing and uniting, procreating all the love that exists right now.—*'I' Will Lift Up Mine Eyes.*

I am presenting to you the reader a new Metaphysic called **Life**. I am suggesting that Life is only expressed in **Man and Woman Balance**. This metaphysic presents to us our fundamental ***Existential (Sexual) Surrender Into Spiritual Procreation.*** You see, "<u>Our</u> **purpose together is to bring the Message of Man and Woman Balance to Planet Earth!**"

Now, you might be asking, who does this guy think he is, Jesus Christ incarnate? Well, allow me to state "I'm just a Man who happens to believe in Woman." That will have to be good enough for that is **Life** itself.

The Man and Woman Spiritual Center © 1990; Illumination © 1990, 2010

The Man and Woman Spiritual Center is only expressed in an actual touch between a man and a woman. It cannot be expressed in any other way. That touch may range from a momentary conscious recognition to a full embrace, but a touch, one to another, it is. The Spiritual Center is not expressed through belief, pledge, worship, ritual, or the paying of alms. It is not something that can be institutionalized, dogmatized, or ratified. There isn't any prescribed path to take, master to follow, or status to attain for its expression. There is only a man and a woman, touching and expressing creation together.

The Touch—You cannot seek it. No, first you must hold it within yourself. And how do you do that? By seeing/feeling this perfection within another. And you do so when you hold to the balance of equal and opposite (the New Trinity) with another. The New Trinity is simply an offering/touch of heart and soul, man to woman and woman to man.

Meditation As Spiritual Procreation © 2023

Your love, at this precise moment, is a perfect love, as is mine. And there is no fear in love. (1 John 4:18: *There is no fear in love: but perfect love casteth out fear: because fear hath torment. He that feareth is not made perfect in love.*) Your love, as is mine, is a balanced love which is a perfect love. How can we know this? Because the Holy Trinity has been redefined to include, a priori, the female force of creation, to stand equal and opposite to the male force of creation. This is the balance. There is no other balance. And so **we together**, male and female, walk the path of the Savior. Salvation is a dual encounter. It is *A Love Perfected: The Coming Age of Spiritual Procreation*. This understanding, this Truth, this Courage, this Grace comprises the **healing of our souls** as we now come home to the balance with one another that has always resided in the longing in our souls. More specifically, we come into sexual balance with our Eternal Other Half.

The Miracle of Life*

**The miracle of life is that the whole
of the universe/life is based on
male and female procreant love without
which there wouldn't be any universe/life!**

*The Prime Movers: The Sovereigncy of Man and Woman, 2015

For those of you who still doubt, and it is difficult for anyone to give up their embedded belief system, a belief system being held on to ever so tightly that if anyone dares threaten it well, beware. Isn't all the conflict in the world simply due to our effort to stand above another in life. "I come first," we proclaim. We may not shout it from the rooftops; we may just hold it silently within—but it is there.

John 15:13: *Greater love hath no man than this, that a man lay down his life for his friends.*

The Flag of the Universe!

I came across the writing *Jesus the Son of Man* by Kahlil Gibran in my early twenties. I have had the opportunity to read it again in my seventies. Both times I was <u>touched</u>. Below is a quote from this great writing.

Kahlil Gibran – Jesus the Son of Man © 1928
Assaph Called the Orator of Tyre

"The Greek and the Roman orators spoke to their listeners of life as it seemed to the mind. The Nazarene spoke of a longing that lodged in the heart.

"They saw life with eyes only a little clearer than yours and mine. He saw life in the light of God.

"I often think that He spoke to the crowd as a mountain would speak to the plain.

"And in his speech there was a power that was not commanded by the orators of Athens or of Rome."

The Touch, one unto another, that is the Christ moment. That is the *"light of God."*

And to you the reader. Thank you for taking the time to read this writing. I have included an Epilogue which follows to maybe help anchor this writing deep within, but this is the formal end. And so, if I may, let us conclude with a quote from the American poet Emily Dickinson.

Emily Dickinson (1830-1886) *Selected Poems*

"This is my letter to the world,
That never wrote to me,—
The simple news that nature told,
With tender majesty.
"Her message is committed
To hands I cannot see;
For love of her, sweet countrymen,
Judge tenderly of me!"

Epilogue: Meditations for Deepening Love

Aphorisms for the New Age of Man and Woman

Family – The Force to Save the Planet

The Light at the End of the Mind

The Faith That Moves Mountains

The First Pair

Aphorisms

for the New Age

of Man and Woman

*Love is the only state of existence
between Male and Female.*

The following aphorisms are listed to provide one with the principles necessary to conceptualize and experience the man and woman relationship as the one creative process of existence in which each of us are embedded.

1. *Male-Female is.*
-In the non-beginning never-ending is male-female.

2. *Male and Female are.*
-Male-Female divide, separating into the distinct sexualities of male and female that they are.

3. *Life is Male and Female.*
-Separated, male and female express their distinct sexualities that they are to each other.

4. *Death is Male-Female.*
-Male and female unite into the rest of male-female.

5. *Birth-Life-Death-Rebirth is Male and Female in dividing-uniting interaction with each other.*
-The division of male-female into male and female is the birth of life. The unification of male and female into male-female is the death of life. The division of male-female into male and female is the rebirth of life.

6. *Eternity is the birth-life-death-rebirth of Male and Female.*
-The interaction of male and female division and unification never began nor will ever end.

7. *Male and Female are eternal to each other, never without each other.*
-Male and female are always in interaction, one sexuality implies the other, eternally.

8. *Male and Female interact due to their desire to do so.*
-The dividing-uniting sexual interaction between male and female is inspired by their creative desire.

9. All desire is sexual desire.
-Sexuality, male or female, is the impetus of desire.

10. Sexual desire is energy or motive force.
-The energy or force of universe is that of sexual desire.

11. All sexual desire is Male desire or Female desire.
-Sexual desire is stipulated by sexuality, it being male or female.

12. All energy is Male energy or Female energy.
-Energy, being sexual desire, is either male or female in force.

13. Male and Female are all that is.
-Male and female comprise the two forces that through their interaction make up all that is.

14. Male is individualization.
-Male is that force which seeks to individualize a form separate and apart from the unity of male-female.

15. Female is unification.
-Female is that force which seeks to unify separate forms together from the division of male and female.

16. Male force is generative.
-The desire of male to divide from the female and individualize form is the compressive effort that creates form, male out of female.

17. Female force is radiative.
-The desire of female to unite with male and unify separate forms is the expansive rest that decreates form, male into female.

18. Male and Female create-decreate-recreate all that is.
-The interaction of male and female is that which creates through compressive effort the individual forms of male and female, and decreates those forms through expansive rest to again recreate...

19. Male desire creates Female.

-Through the male desire to individualize a form apart from female, female, too, is brought into form in relationship to male.

20. Female desire decreates Male.
-Through the female desire to unite separated forms, male, too, is taken out of form into male-female.

21. Male desire is securitive.
-Through the male desire to hold separate form, male as to female, life is secured.

22. Female desire is reproductive.
-Through the female desire to unite separate forms together, male-female, life is reproduced.

23. Male secures Female for the reproduction of Female.
-The male, in his desire to hold separate form, secures female form so that he in turn may be reproduced in form by female.

24. Female reproduces Male for the security of Male.
-The female, in her desire to unite separate forms together, reproduces male form so that she in turn may be secured in form by male.

25. Male and Female create-decreate-recreate together.
 -Male and female together comprise the purpose and process of creation. Neither of them alone can bring forth the birth-life-death-rebirth continuum of all that is. The two forces must interact, and do so as to their nature, dividing and uniting together.

26. Male and Female exist in the state of rhythmic balanced interchange.
-The male force and the female force are equally essential to the existence of either of them. The two forces of creation hold absolute balance together.

27. Love is the rhythmic balanced interchange between Male and Female.

-Love is manifested in the balance of male and female, dividing and uniting together, bringing forth the creation-decreation-recreation of all that is.

28. *Love is eternally creative.*
-The male and female rhythmic balanced interchange never began nor will ever end but is always creating, manifesting love one to the other.

29. *Love is the only state of existence between Male and Female.*
-Male and female are in love together, right now and forever.

Family

The Force To Save The Planet

Family is not physical but metaphysical!

What would you do or whom would you turn to if it became apparent to you that this planet earth was under assault? Or maybe it should be asked, what would it take for you to believe that planet earth is under assault? Would you need to see some army taking over your town or home? Maybe you would first have to be hauled away to some prison camp. But what if suddenly your marriage dissolved or your children turned their backs on you and you found yourself left with nothing? Would that get your attention? Perhaps the real assault on planet earth is not coming from some overt source but is coming from within. Perhaps it is a spiritual assault that we almost cannot see, an assault going right into our core and yet we are nearly defenseless to do anything about it. I would suggest to you that it is an assault on that thing that is most dear to us. The assault is a spiritual one on the family.

But, it must be asked, why would anyone want to assault the family? Isn't the family that order of life that allows for life? The family is that one man and one woman unit that when united in marriage is the base and stability of procreation. We might say that all life comes through family. It is the balance (equal and opposite) of male and female that holds the family together such that children can be born and raised to continue the play of creation. Without family, there isn't any hope for any of us. In short, the family is life.

So again, it must be asked, why would anyone want to assault the family? You would think that all of us would do everything we can to support this institution. Yet it is being assaulted on all sides. Don't we hear today how the monogamous marriage is outdated, how we as men and women don't really need the other sex in our lives; how sex is whatever feels good irrespective of commitment and procreation; how in the name of our "sovereign" choice it is morally acceptable to kill unborn children; or how babies are being created only for their stem cells or organs, etc.? Or, maybe your child comes home from school one day to inform you that he or she is "gay." Or, the state takes your child from you and your spouse because the state does not like how you are raising your child. So you turn to your church for help and support only to find that your minister, pastor, or priest (of your IRS-registered church) can only tell you to ask for forgiveness. Suddenly, you realize that no one is there to stand up for the family. Why?

May I suggest that the assault upon the family is imposed by the threat the family presents to the powers-that-be. The threat is one of sovereigncy. (Sovereigncy means co-sovereignty; a sexual procreative two, i.e., a male and a female.) Family is the sovereign center of the universe. It is sovereign by its procreative nature. (It takes a man and a woman to make a baby.) As the sovereign center, nothing stands over or under it. Family is that one living entity that breaks the master/slave hierarchy the powers-that-be use to enslave us. Family leaves us accountable for procreation, leaves us free to pursue our own happiness (earn and own), and presents to us the inner strength to stand up for and defend the family we comprise.

For those of us who want the family to survive, and with it all life, we must first understand the nature of this assault. As I have mentioned, it is a spiritual assault. The battle is for the soul of man and woman. The attempt is to get a man and a woman to believe in anything else but family, to believe that a committed, sacred marriage between one man and one woman is but an illusion. In my view, there are generally three areas from which this assault is coming.

The first direction of this assault is from the church. By the church, I mean any institution of any religion. You might think that if anything stands for the family it is the church. But the church does not hold the family as being the sacred and sovereign center of all things. Historically, it has often supported patriarchy.* The church holds (a one-force) "God" as the sacred and sovereign entity of which we are called to submit. We are told we cannot find our salvation or eternal life except through "God" or his son (Christianity) or that the eternal (singular force) Self is within us individually (Hinduism), etc. Nowhere is it mentioned that a man and a woman come together as eternally mated (procreative) pairs and that our sole salvation is in understanding the reality of our existential need for each other. In other words, in all of our religions today, the church places its sanctity above and before the family.

We are to choose Jesus or the Self, etc., before our husband or wife. Can you see how this undermines marriage and family at the spiritual level? Spiritually speaking, in our religions of today, man and woman are not primary. We have never understood their eternal/procreative balance together. As such, we undercut the spiritual base of family and place it in second position. It is not to stand on itself. If the family were to stand on itself that, of course, would undermine the (hierarchical) "authority" of the church and the alms to the church would dry up. And thus, we see the real reason that the church cannot allow the family to be sovereign.

*Patriarchy is the imbalance of male domination. Today churches, primarily in the West, in the name of equality, are moving to a feminist imbalance.

Another assault upon the family comes from the state or what I also refer to as the nation-state. The ideology (religion) of the nation-state is that of secular humanism. Secular humanism holds that all people are equal under the state. In this case, the state is the sovereign or leviathan master supposedly acting in the name of the people. Secular humanism has its roots in the Dialectical Materialism of Karl Marx and others. Today, it is known under the banner of democracy. In secular humanism, there isn't any mention of the necessity of the family. Men and women are viewed as singular or independent of each other (and, in essence, work for the state). "We can stand on ourselves alone," they would claim as they all clamor for the state to give to them the handout as if it were their right. Of course, the state can only provide what it itself has first taken (stolen) from some poor sap who is just trying to support his family. The state retains its power over the people by promising the handout and at the same time keeping the people in need. Like the church, its motive to undermine the family is economic. If the family stood on its own, which the state cannot allow it to do, the state's only task would be to protect the unalienable rights of all and provide for none. Then, the politicians might have to get an honest job.

The third assault upon the family that I want to mention comes from the feminist/homosexual coalition. The attempt of the feminist/homosexual coalition is to redefine the family structure itself. Rather than the basis of a family being that structure of marriage between a man and a woman that is procreative to life, a new definition of family is to arise. This "new family" would consist of anything people consented to. There could be homosexual "families," bisexual "families," or transgender "families" but gender distinction between one man and one woman as we have known it would no longer be the defining characteristic of family. We may still have man and woman families but that would just be another choice among the many choices available. The intention of the feminist/homosexual coalition is to deny and destroy the essential necessity of the one man and one woman family as that procreative center of all things. They call for "reproductive rights" so they can sidestep the reality that it takes a man and a woman to make a baby. They advocate abortion as a "life" choice to create the appearance of freedom from sexual (man and woman) interdependence. And they seek to "teach" children their ways of "love" that deny the essential essence of procreative love and leave a man and a woman spiritually empty inside.

The attempt to undermine or destroy the family is the attempt to undermine or destroy life itself. Without the one man and one woman family as that center point of all creation, we are doomed. Given this reality, I again must ask, why? Why is the church, the state, and the feminist/homosexual coalition, or anyone else, trying to undermine/destroy the family? Don't these people know that they themselves cannot exist without it? Yet the assault continues. Why?

The answer to this assault upon the family is solely yours to discover. And discover it you will, once you have made the commitment to support the one man and one woman marriage and family as if your own life is dependent upon it, and dependent on nothing else. And supporting the family is all any of us need to do to save this planet for, you see, the family is nothing other than that exact procreative order from which all things revolve in perfect (sexual/spiritual) balance. *Family is not physical but metaphysical!* The family (in its two-way sexual process) is not just the "one force" to save the planet, it is the only force to save the planet. Life only exists in the balance of family.

Family

The Light
at the End
of the Mind

It simply is what it is and cannot be what it is not.

The light at the end of the mind illuminates the mind with all clarity. Clarity—a purity of constant realization that this light could only reside at the end of the mind. After all ideas have come into awareness—without an answer. After all action from these ideas have been taken—to no avail. After all hope has been lost, and finally admitted to, here comes the last idea. Yes, the light at the end of the mind is but an *idea*. An idea that is a *word*--a word that contains all the meaning of life and illuminates the mind with the understanding that has been missing since the dawn of consciousness. The light at the end of the mind is the last idea to be brought to consciousness. It is the final idea of all mankind. It is the one idea all have been waiting for. It is the one idea that will organize all disorder out of the mind. It is the one idea that will free the spirit of all envy. It is the one idea that will relieve the heart of all burden. But this idea will only do that if it is put in its proper perspective as the single and center point of all existence. There is to be no greater idea. There is to be no more significant understanding. There is to be no more enduring truth. Not that we or anyone is to bow down to this idea. It stands only as the central organizing factor of all thought and action, bringing clarity to our lives and everything we do or aspire to. The light at the end of the mind, that exists as an idea and is known through a word, is now ready to illuminate a mind.

The light at the end of the mind is not necessarily a new idea. It has been heard before. But never has it been uttered in its proper context. Never has it been known as the final idea, as the greatest idea, as an idea that encompasses the whole of the understanding, bringing all order to that understanding. The idea, cherished by few, has conveniently been relegated to second tier by mankind in his/her religious, political, and sexual belief systems. The great religious and philosophical books presenting the great ideas of mankind forget to mention it. Your author remembers seeing it only one time.* You, the reader, when you hear this idea, may think you already know about it, that you have superior knowledge and are not moved. But let me impress upon you, this idea has yet to be understood in its *spiritual* significance. I assure you, you will not know what that significance is. You must allow the idea into your mind free of your own preconceptions and let it do its work. *Let it* *work in you.* If left to do its work, it will reorganize your mind and free your heart such that a light will begin to grow, and glow, within you—the light at the end of the mind.

Leaves of Grass—Walt Whitman, 1855

    The idea that is a word that exists as the light at the end of the mind only exists at the end of the mind. If this idea does not crush you with its simplicity, if it does not freeze you with its purity, if it does not release you in it universality, if it does not center you in its totality, if it does not extend you in its density, if it does not embrace you with its clarity, please do not enter its gates. I know you want to read on and see what this *word* is but don't, for this word only exists at the end of the mind. You can only see it from that vantage point. If you haven't yet *lost your own mind,* don't read on. If you haven't yet had *your spirit crushed,* don't read on. If you haven't yet *lost all faith* in the immensity of faith, don't read on. If you haven't yet discovered it was never about you or not about you, don't read on. If you are not ready for instant enlightenment, don't read on—the light at the end of the mind is the brightest of lights. It has already blinded all those who cannot see.

    The light at the end of the mind is but an idea that is a word. It does not need an explanation. In fact, it cannot be explained. It is what is called *self-evident.* Its meaning will be instantly known. The light at the end of the mind has always been known. Admitted to or not, agreed to or not, it will be recognized as truth. To those of you who have questions, none will be answered. To those of you who have doubts—they are your own. To those of you who speak ill of this word, you will feel a darkness surround you. This is not personal nor is this stated as some absolute judgment. You see, there isn't any subjective compromise to be had. We just are not able to place our subjective desires into the metaphysical structure and constraints of the universe. Subjective compromise has always been our downfall. The light at the end of the mind cannot compromise. *It simply is what it is and cannot be what it is not.* The light at the end of the mind is always and only what it is. It has always been what it is and has never been what it is not. It will always be what it is and will never be what it is not. The light at the end of the mind is, and can only be, an idea that is a word. That word is *procreant*.

The
Faith
That Moves
Mountains

The faith is the spiritual birth between two (procreative) hearts.

Let thou thy voice speak unto thee—of the faith that moves mountains. I now tell you, faith is but a word that also means the *truth*. It is not faith in itself that moves mountains. It is the truth and the faith in the truth that moves mountains. Faith stands on the truth. "So, what is the truth?" you ask. Let me first speak to you about what is the mountain. The mountain is the belief system(s) the world is now holding. It is the belief systems of the world that are blocking truth from entering into the heart of mankind. What is your belief? *Let it go.* You must let it go.

"Ah, but that is not so easy," you say. Indeed, our identities are tied around our belief systems. "Show me your truth, then I will decide," you exclaim. But, I must ask, where is the faith in that? You must *let it go* before I can speak to you of the truth. "How is that done?" you ask. "One just can't let go of one's belief." Do you not trust in yourself? Do you fear you might lose yourself? Do you even know the truth of yourself? Surrender, my friend. Surrender it all. Your belief system will no longer serve you.

"Well, just who are you? Why should I believe you?" you ask. Let me tell you who I once was. Once I was a Christian. Once I was a Jew. Once I was a Hindu, a Muslim, a Buddhist, a Mormon, a Transcendentalist, a Paganist, an Atheist, a Humanist, a Nationalist, a Racist, a Libertarian, a Communist, a Republican, a Democrat, a Feminist, a Bisexual, a Homosexual, a Transsexual, a Cross-dresser, and many more things as well. All of those "identities" died within me--I even thought for a moment there wasn't any "me." And then, in an instant, I suddenly knew what never could be taught. You see, the truth is not some concept held in the "singular mind" where one can then say "I know." The truth is a *living* activity. It is that process we call life. And as is the case with all life, it must be *born*.

"The truth is born! How is that suppose to work?" you ask. The truth is born just as a baby is born. We call the process *procreation*. In procreation, a man and a woman give their lives to each other. The man gives his security (seed) to the woman and the woman gives her reproduction (womb) to the man. They are giving to each other their essential sexual selves in a moment of eternal surrender. We call this *love*. And from this love a union forms which begins a new process of division into a new sexual form, male or female, to be born into life. It is this process of begetting life that is the truth. Each time a new baby is born, the truth is expressed. Each time a man and a woman touch in the love that is the procreation of their spirits, the truth is expressed. Our faith in life, the faith that moves mountains, is the faith in this truth that is the expression of divine *procreant* love.

"But how can this be?" you ask. "Not everyone is making babies." It is the spirit of procreation to which I speak. Each child comes into life under the spirit of procreation. Each child feels within his or her heart a calling for their opposite other through which they together will carry on the *lineage of life*. As adults we live through our children, wanting our children themselves to become adults and have children of their own. As grandparents we further live through our children's children...and so on. The procreant urge fosters all life and never leaves any life. As we mature that urge takes on spiritual proportions—and beauty is brought into the understanding. The eternal procreation of a man and a woman continues beyond child-bearing years to include the procreation of the eternal itself. The eternal exists only as it is procreated, moment-by-moment, out of the surrender/love of a man to a woman and a woman to a man. Whatever is your current status in life, hold this *procreant* love in your heart and let it be your guide.

"But...what ...." I see that you do not believe. *Because of your unbelief: for verily I say unto you, If ye have faith as a grain of mustard seed, ye shall say unto this mountain, Remove hence to yonder place; and it shall remove; and nothing shall be impossible unto you.* Might not the mountain be within you? The mountain is our own (singular) belief system. You, and I, can remove the mountain from within ourselves right now by our faith. *The faith is the spiritual birth between two (procreative) hearts.* Take a moment and remove this mountain to a yonder place. "How might I do that?" you ask. By praying, *in faith,* the *Eternal Prayer.* Pray the *Eternal Prayer* to your eternal (equal and opposite) other half right now and know that your mountain is forevermore removed.

The Eternal Prayer

My blessed love, please come into my heart and live in me.
Allow me, as well, to come into your heart and live in you. Let us,
from this moment on, live in each other's hearts,
our love together being our guide, shining a light for all
to see that life is held simply in "our" balance together.

The

First Pair

The First Pair has come!

The First Pair has come! We thought the return would be through Jesus or some Avatar type. It wasn't. We thought there would be a great rejoicing—some final salvation. There wasn't. We thought the return would bring peace on earth. It didn't. Certainly the return would at least better our plights. It didn't even do that. So what then was the return, what did it do? Perhaps--could it?--touch one heart.

Man: We, my beloved wife and I, have come forth to unite together that we may have child. If you understand what I have just said, you understand all things.

Woman: Our child, created out of our love--let that be the light that shines for us our way.

Man: If you don't understand what my wife and I just said, let me illuminate. We, the *First Pair*, are what you have, heretofore, called God. We are the first cause, the divine principle and purpose, the primal force(s), the source of all creation. All that is exists through us, our love.

Woman: The spirit of our love connects us all—from the first man and woman to the last which again becomes the first. It is this spirit that is the *Holy Spirit*. We, the *First Pair*, speak to you through our hearts.

Man: The first creation, our child, came from us out of the balance that we together comprise. Please understand, *balance* is the first principle. You cannot circumvent it. Balance always comprises an equal and opposite two—a man and a woman, *primordially*. That is its definition.

Woman: From our balance a child is born. Our balance is our love.

Man: Within the balance is the *procreant*. We, man and woman, are procreant *together*. We are only procreant with each other. Procreation is our eternal lineage. Our balance, as a procreant moment between two equal but opposite *sexed* forces, comprises the eternal.

Woman: The *First Pair* is always eternal. Our love that flows through our balance is eternal love. Our love always exists for our child. As it will never die; it sustains all life at all times.

Man: We, the *First Pair*, exist in the heart or soul of all things directing all things. Balance is our guide. Balance is our law. No one, not even us, can circumvent the *sexual balance* between a man and a woman.

Woman: Your anguish is that you seek and cannot find. Until you hold the balance of our love in your hearts, you can never find. When you do you will know that you *two* can never be lost for you, too, are the *First Pair*, knowing your own love together even before the beginning.

Man: I, man, divide the one.

Woman: I, woman, unite the two.

Man: We, dividing from and uniting with each other, *together* constitute the source of all creation. Not alone; not with something else. Not through anything else. Your life hinges on the *procreant balance* you hold with your eternal other half, just as does mine.

Woman: Don't despair. Rejoice. You, right now, can invite your eternal other half into your heart. I remember the day well when my husband and I said our prayer and took our vows together. That wonderful moment lives in our hearts to this day. We say our prayer and vows together each moment, every day. That is how it *lives*.

Man: Look at us, a man and a woman. What would you have us say? We stand not apart from you. We claim no dimension greater than you. We hold out our hands to you in the consciousness that we, the *First Pair*, can only shine the love to you that arises out of the love we have for our child.

Woman: My sisters, can you feel yourself holding your child in your arms, that child created by your husband and yourself? Is not that the greatest of all miracles?

Man: And brothers, feel the pride you have in securing your family. Every one of you, together with your wives, is surely the *First Pair*. May you take this stand for life.

Woman: The *First Pair* is the only stand my husband takes. And he gives this all to me. I receive all so that we, the *First Pair*, may be reproduced out of my spirit-womb once again. I am woman. All things born out of me come back into me to be reborn out of me.... For surely this is our truth.

Man: To woman I give my life. To woman I make my surrender. To woman I embrace my eternal life as man, only and always with her eternal life as woman. Together we, man and woman, stand on our life eternal.

Woman: How could it be any other way?

Man: The *First Pair*, an original idea, now being differentiated into consciousness as the source of all consciousness by a *First Pair*, is, from this moment on, delineated to be existent at the soul of all things, guiding all things to a universal awareness of 'itself' (as a two procreant forces/*First Pair*), an awareness that from this day forth can never be undone.

Woman: And there is love.

Author: Christopher Alan Anderson (1950-) received the basis of his education from the University of Science and Philosophy, Swannanoa, Waynesboro, Virginia. He resides in the transcendental/romantic tradition, that vein of spiritual creativity of the philosopher and poet. His quest has been to define and express an eternal *romantic* reality from which a man and a woman could *together* stand and create a *living* universe. Mr. Anderson began these writings in 1971. The first writings were published in 1985.

Writings by the Author:

The Divine Touch: A New Creation for Life!

Humanitarian Project: Man and Woman Balance

Etheric Materialization Into Form!

Selected Writings—Volume 3: A New Trinity

Channeling the Eternal Woman

The Case Against Man and Woman – A Philosophy on Trial

Meditations for Deepening Love

Let There Be Life!

Meditation as Spiritual Procreation

Spiritual Healing of Our Eternal Souls for All Time

The Man and Woman Manifesto: What We Believe!

Reflections on Light: From a Homeless Shelter

The Prime Movers: The Sovereigncy of Man and Woman

The Metaphysics of Sex …in a Changing World!

Wealth Plus+ Empowering Your Everyday!

The 2008 - 2009 Articles

To Cassandra—Early Years

Man, Woman, and God

The Man and Woman Relationship: A New Center for the Universe

Illumination

Selected Writings—Volume 2

The Discovery of Life

The Man and Woman Manifesto: Let the Revolution Begin

Psychotherapy As If Life Really Mattered

The Universal Religion: The Final Destiny of Mankind

The Truth Revealed: My Answer to the World

Healing In The Light & The Art and Practice of Creativity

www.ingramcontent.com/pod-product-compliance
Lightning Source LLC
Chambersburg PA
CBHW070546160426

43199CB00014B/2399